CHALLENGE AND CONFORMITY

Challenge and Conformity

*Studies in the Interaction of Christianity
and the World of Today*

BY

KENNETH SCOTT LATOURETTE

*Sterling Professor of Missions and Oriental History, Emeritus
and Associate Fellow of Berkeley College in Yale University*

HARPER & BROTHERS PUBLISHERS

NEW YORK

To

Hugh George Anderson

unfailingly helpful companion

in pilgrimage

CONTENTS

PREFACE

How does Christianity respond to the varying environments in which it is found? To what extent does it conform to them? What is their response to it? How far does it transform them? These are questions to the discussion of which many volumes could be devoted. Indeed, they could not be adequately dealt with by a work of lesser dimensions. To one who would understand the part which Christianity plays in the human scene they are of major importance.

It is not the purpose of the brief chapters which follow to essay that full-scale treatment. In several other books the author has sought to deal with one or another aspect of the broad field. He does not intend again even to summarize what he has said in them. What is endeavoured here is to look at some features of one phase of the subject. How far is Christianity conforming to the contemporary world? In conforming is Christianity doing so in such fashion that it is weakening or losing the essence of its Gospel? On the other hand, is it so responding that its Gospel is being released from crippling integuments inherited from its accommodation to earlier environments and so to fresh expressions of its power? How is the contemporary world responding to Christianity? In what ways is it being shaped by Christianity?

To deal even with these questions in satisfactory fashion would demand at least a large tome. The twentieth-century world is varied and complex. A vast, world-wide revolution is in progress which is affecting all mankind. It is issuing from "Christendom," where Christianity has longest had its course. Christianity is represented in almost every people, tribe, and nation, sometimes by small minorities, sometimes by large ones. In several nations Christianity has the professed allegiance of the large majority. A number of peoples among whom it has been present for many centuries have commonly been regarded as Christian. This is especially the situation in Europe. But in most lands which constitute what we once thought of as Christendom the past two centuries or more have seen movements away from the faith. So strikingly have they mounted in recent decades that many are declaring that we are entering the post-Christian era. However, even in these lands, after seeming defeats Christianity is displaying marked vitality and among minorities it is vigorous and is responding to threats with new movements in thought and deed. In numbers of other lands and peoples Christianity is spreading. Indeed, never has it or any other religion been as widely extended geographically, as deeply rooted among as many peoples, and as much a force in the life of all mankind as in the mid-twentieth century. In past centuries Christianity has shown marked capacity to adapt itself to new and changing civilizations. It is continuing to do so. Amid rapidly shifting scenes, in the midst of revolutions which are in part its fruit, it is persisting and spreading, and it is preserving the Gospel, the central core upon which its vitality depends.

The ensuing pages are deliberately limited to three groups of areas. One is Europe, where Christianity long had its chief centres and where now it is undergoing major tests which threaten its continued existence. The other two are portions of the globe in which in our day Christianity has been experiencing its most rapid numerical growth. One of the latter is the United States. Here church membership is mounting both among elements of the population—Indians, Negroes, and small enclaves from the Far East—whose ancestors were not Christian and among those of Christian ancestry who in the course of migration from Europe or from one section of the country to another have been partially de-Christianized. This is of peculiar importance because of the large place which the churches of the United States are having in the ecumenical scene and in the spread of the faith in other lands. The other area is in what we have traditionally called the non-Christian world. Here, with some exceptions, Christianity is registering progress in numbers of adherents, in leadership, and in some of its effects. The exceptions are a few remote lands where Christianity has been planted, even if at all, in the face of great difficulties, among peoples who have long been Moslem, and China, North Korea, and parts of Indochina, where Communism has recently dealt severe blows to churches which until its achievement of political control were growing, some of them rapidly. Progress in the non-Christian world is at varying rates. In a few regions World War II and its aftermath have brought reverses. In general, however, the course of Christianity has been forward, whether in Africa south of the Sahara, in India, in Indonesia, or in smaller lands. Here, in the non-Occidental world, Christianity is facing a crucial test. Christianity has long been associated with the Occident. Yet by its genius it is for all men. Can it be effectively and permanently planted outside the Occident? If so, can it there preserve its essential character, or will it so conform to its new environments that it will be denatured?

In as brief a space as these chapters must necessarily be we cannot discuss fully the response to Christianity and of Christianity even in these areas. We may, however, hope to suggest certain outstanding features in such fashion as to be of help to those who have the interest or the time for only a cursory survey and to those who wish an introduction to more detailed study and investigation.

Portions of this book were given in the spring of 1954 as lectures at the Universities of Copenhagen, Aarhus, Uppsala, and Oslo, and in the theological school of Bethel bei Bielefeld. To the generous courtesy of the faculties who arranged for them and to the audiences who listened to them, delivered as they were in an alien tongue, the author is profoundly grateful.

The author is in continued and thankful debt to Mrs. Charles T. Lincoln for skilfully typing this, as she has more than a score of earlier volumes, large and small, and for her suggestions as to literary style.

The author is also deeply grateful to Hugh George Anderson, who went with him to Europe and who by his companionship and thoughtful and understanding assistance lightened the tedium and burdens of travel and immeasurably enriched the pilgrimage.

CHALLENGE AND CONFORMITY

CHAPTER I

The Issues in Their Historical Perspective

THE questions to which we are addressing ourselves are by no means new. They arise in connexion with all religions. Each individual makes his own interpretation of the faith which he professes. That profession may be only nominal. It may be through passive or semi-passive conformation to the social group in which he finds himself. Even when nominal and passive, those attitudes are reflected in religion as he conceives it and practices it. Moreover, his response is partly shaped by the cultural environment, both by the past of that environment and by current changes in it. Thus Islam, one of the seemingly most inflexible of religions and presumably bound to the letter of the Koran, has been modified by tradition, by the several cultures of the peoples who have accepted it, and by changing climates of opinion. The Islam of Persia is not precisely that of Arabia. That of Indonesia has variations from them both. Islam as held and taught by Averroes differed profoundly from that as believed and propagated by Aurangzeb. Hinduism is characterized by both flexibility and tolerance on the one hand, with capacity to embrace in its wide fold many differing and even contradictory views, and on the other hand by intolerance of systems and individuals who will not accommodate themselves to it. Judaism has taken many forms across the years and has varied greatly among individuals, and that in spite of a core of orthodoxy which has been standard for many centuries. Buddhism is notable for the fashion in which it has responded to the many cultures into which it has moved. Indeed, evidence of the continuing vitality of a religion seems to be in what look like contradictory manifestations. On the one hand are the incorporation of elements from different cultures and changing climates of opinion and stimulus to individuals and groups to initiate fresh movements with drastic modifications and innovations. On the other hand is the persistence of distinguishing prime characteristics which are never fully relinquished. Unless it has both these qualities a religion has neither a wide spread nor a long life.

Christianity has been notable for its combination of the two. It has been flexible in its ability to adapt itself to many cultures. This arises in part from its beginning. Jesus wrote no book. He spoke much, but most of his teaching which was remembered and is preserved in the Gospels was in the framework of a particular occasion in reply to a request, a question, a challenge from a critic, the attitude of the ones with whom he was talking, or an incident. With notable exceptions his teaching was not in systematic form. Nor did he dictate it to an amanuensis. It was therefore not a law with rigid categories. His sayings have been used to support varied and often contradictory economic, political, and social theories and systems. Then, too, Jesus seems to have given little thought to an organization to perpetuate his mission. Certainly we have no report of his outlining a structure for the Church, and only in two places, and they merely in one Gospel, are we told that the word "Church" was on his lips. During at least the first generation of his followers ecclesiastical organization was, quite understandably, fluid. This made for adaptability.

Moreover, Christianity has spread more widely and among more different cultures than has any other religion, especially in the past five centuries and notably in the present century. This brings with it an added danger to such accommodation that the heart of the Gospel will be lost.

It is not surprising, therefore, that what in the broadest sense of that term can be called Christianity has taken many forms. These have in part been in response to the environment.

From the formative era we recall the several varieties of Jewish Christians which emerged in the first two centuries, men and women who wished to remain within their ancestral faith and its practices and yet to make room for Jesus. We remember, also in those centuries, the many Gnostic systems, numbers of which gave a place to Jesus, and we remind ourselves that Gnosticism seems to have been an expression of a religious temper of the times and that not all its forms took account of Jesus. Those Gnostic teachers who made room for him were attempting to acclimatize him, to think through what he meant in terms of current cosmogenies and cosmologies. The theologies which the majority of Christians came to regard as orthodox employed terms and concepts which they found in the philosophies of the Græco-Roman world. In its structure the early Catholic Church reflected the political organization of the Roman Empire. In many important respects through the centuries the Roman Catholic Church has been the heir of that empire and is a continuation of its temper— with its use of the language of Rome, its desire to bring the world under its sway, and its stress on law. Others of the severed branches of the Catholic Church of the first few centuries have also kept the administration by dioceses which was an adaptation paralleling what was seen in the Empire. There have been and are scholars who would have us believe that what we call Christianity conformed so extensively to the ancient world that little remained of its primitive content. Some would contend that it became simply another of the many mystery religions which were then popular and that in it the Jesus who walked and talked in Galilee and Judea was made to give way to a Jesus of myth. Some declare that the cult of the Virgin owes much to pagan goddesses, that many local patron saints were really pagan gods under new names, and that the great Christian feasts borrowed so much from pagan festivals, even as to dates, that what in them came from Christ was either lost or hopelessly distorted. We remember how much Christian ethics were and are indebted to Stoicism. We recall how Oriental and Hellenistic dualism entered into Christian thought and practice with the conception that matter, including flesh, is evil, and that salvation consists in deliverance from matter and entering into the realm of pure spirit. Here was a powerful force in the origin, development, and continuation of monasticism.

As we make our way in retrospect through the centuries which have elapsed since the disintegration of the Roman Empire we see again and again ways in which Christianity has reflected the successive environments in which it has existed. We remember the influence of Plato and Aristotle upon the theologies of the Middle Ages. We note that Augustine, whom most of these theologies held in high esteem, was a converted Platonist and that, partly through him, there has been a strong strain of Platonism in Christian thought. In the Middle Ages and later, much of Christian mysticism was profoundly influenced by the writings ascribed to Dionysius the Areopagite, and through them Neoplatonism made a deep mark on it. During and after the Middle Ages secular monarchs sought to dominate the Church in their realms and to use it for their

purposes. In this they were eventually aided by the rising tides
of nationalism and there came into being national churches,
some within the Roman Catholic Church, some in Eastern
Europe, Western Asia, and Egypt, and others within Protestantism. The fashion in which the geographical line of division
in Western Europe between the Roman Catholic Church and
Protestantism approximates the northern boundary of the
Roman Empire seems to give support to the thesis that the
Roman Catholic Church is really a partially Christianized ver-
sion of *Romanitas* and that Protestantism is the reaction of
the Germanic peoples to Christianity. This thesis is an over-
simplification, but there is enough evidence to support it to
keep us from dismissing it lightly. In Germany powerful arch-
bishoprics sprang in part from the fertile mind of Otto the
Great, who saw them, non-hereditary as they were and so subject to partial control by the King, as aids to the central
authority to counterbalance the lay principalities whose rulers,
recruited through heredity, could be formidable rivals to the
monarch. The *Landeskirchen* of Germany reflect the former
political divisions of that realm. The subordination of the
Church to the state which has characterized the Orthodox
Churches is in no small degree to be traced to the long persistence of the Roman Empire in the East after its collapse in
the West and the consequent continuation of the pre-Christian
tradition of its control of religion. The loyalty of the Irish to
the Roman Catholic faith has been in large part because the
Roman Catholic Church was long the one institution which
was theirs as against their English overlords and the latter's
state church, a branch of the Anglican Communion. It has
been a symbol and tie of Irish nationalism. To some extent the
inclusive character of the Church of England stems from the
desire of the first Elizabeth to hold her kingdom together
against foreign and domestic foes and to employ the Church

to that end. Much of the prolonged and current weakness of the Roman Catholic Church in Latin America can be traced to the enforced subordination of that church in colonial days to the Spanish and Portuguese Crowns. Latin-American Catholicism has therefore been anæmic. To this day it does not supply enough clergy to meet the needs of its constituency.

Yet, with all of the responsiveness of Christianity to its environment, there has been in it a central core. Many attempts have been made to define that core. Out of them have come the historic creeds to which the large majority of Christians have long subscribed. From them have arisen the confessions of faith of the Protestant churches. Around them have raged numerous theological battles. In the nineteenth and twentieth centuries we have had debates as to whether the core was corrupted in the early centuries first by Paul and others of the early apostles and then by Greek philosophy. We remember the distinction made between the religion of Jesus and the Jesus of history on the one hand and the religion about Jesus on the other, with the implication that the central core is the first of these alternatives. We are aware that in recent years the trend has been towards regarding that disjunction as untrue to the evidence.

Here is not the place to review and renew the debate. We can, however, and for our purposes we must point out a few facts which are related to it.

In the first place, the great majority of Christians have agreed that the core centres around Jesus Christ. It also includes the Scriptures as recording the preparation for him and as giving us our authoritative record of his birth, life, teachings, crucifixion, resurrection, and ascension and of the teachings of his apostles. Some would hold that the irreducible core includes more than this. A minority would say that it does not embrace that much.

A second fact is that the forms of Christianity which have persisted have stressed that core and have attempted to remain faithful to it. Some have sincerely added to it. However, those forms of the faith which have substantially reduced it have either disappeared or dwindled. The great majority of Christians have subscribed to what is set forth in the Apostles' and Nicene Creeds. They have also held to the creed which bears the name of Chalcedon, with its definition of the place of Jesus Christ in the Godhead and the relation in him of the divine and human. Not all of that majority have subscribed intelligently. Most of them have merely acquiesced. But these definitions of the irreducible core have been officially the belief of the churches to which the majority of Christians have adhered. To be sure, many have been restive, particularly in these later centuries and among Protestants who are members of churches which regard these creeds as standard. They have criticized the creeds as confining Christianity to a strait-jacket forged through controversies now outmoded and fabricated of terminologies and concepts derived from the Greeks and Romans which at best are only partly relevant and which at the worst distort the heart of the Gospel and make it unintelligible to modern man. Yet, it must be reiterated, the majority of Christians belong to churches which hold that the core is to be found in these creeds. Their leaders would acknowledge that Greek terms were used, but at least some of those expert in the history of Christian doctrine hold that in employing these terms the Christians of the early centuries took from the contemporary language and thought with which they were familiar what seemed to them most nearly to express the core of the faith and that in the process they so altered the meaning of the terms as to make them true to that core.

A third fact is that forms of the faith which have departed from the core as set forth in these creeds have not permanently flourished. History is strewn with their graves. The Jewish Christian groups who honoured Jesus as simply the greatest of the prophets died fairly early. The Gnostics, once so popular that for a time they may have enrolled the majority of those who thought of themselves as Christians, but who gave Christ a subordinate place or regarded him as not being both real man and truly God, perished. So did the Marcionites, who taught that the Christ could never have been contaminated with the flesh by becoming man. The Arians, who refused to hold to the full deity of Christ, also disappeared. The Monophysites, who exalt the divine in Christ at the expense of his full humanity, survive, but as encysted minorities. To be sure, in the disappearance or decline of some of these movements other factors than theological ones entered. However, one cause of weakness was a lack of vitality which can be traced to the distortion or abandonment of that core.

In later centuries, it must be noted as a fourth fact, some of the greatest resurgences of power in Christianity have come from earnest attempts to return to the core and to free it from compromising additions and conformations to the world around it. It was that which inspired the great monastic movements. Much the same motive is at the heart of the various forms of Protestantism. Again and again it has been seen in revivals within Protestantism.

As may be gathered from these last paragraphs, the author is committed to what he has here called the core of Christianity. To him that core is the Gospel, the amazing Good News in Jesus Christ who is both God and man and in whom God has supremely entered into history for the redemption of men.

Christianity is a religion. Like other religions, as we see it in the churches it has strong admixtures of human elements. Some of these contradict the Gospel, God's gracious and sufficient gift to men. The history of Christianity is in large part the record of the response of men to the love of God which has manifested itself through the Incarnation, the Cross, the Resurrection, and the Holy Spirit. It is also the record of the love of God operating in various ways, conditioned by cultural inheritance and present forces, many of them antagonistic. In all the multitudinous forms which Christianity has taken on its long pilgrimage in its many cultural settings, its continuing vigour has depended on the degree to which it has been loyal to the Gospel.

This conviction is, if you will, the author's bias. It is from this angle that he enters upon the descriptive summaries of the chapters which follow. Yet he has endeavoured not to allow it to distort his account.

From this historical introduction we move to the areas which are to claim our major attention. We go first to Europe, next to the United States, and then to what we have called the non-Christian or the non-Occidental world.

CHAPTER II

Christianity in the Environment of Present-Day Europe

E UROPE is changing very rapidly. Yet much of the old persists and in spots clashes with the new. Here is one of the commonplaces of the contemporary scene. Europe is both the old world and the new world. It is the centre of Western civilization and the conserver of its values. In it, particularly in Western Europe, has been a dynamic quality. That dynamism has been long at work. We can only speculate as to its source, but among possible explanations is the fact that within it Christianity has longer had relatively free course than in any other part of the world. Whatever its origin, from that dynamism have issued the forces that are working revolutions in the life of all mankind. From it came that remarkable expansion of European peoples which was foreshadowed by the Crusades and the commerce of the eleventh, twelfth, thirteenth, and fourteenth centuries, and which, beginning on a colossal scale in the fifteenth and sixteenth centuries, made European and especially Western European peoples dominant politically and culturally the world over. During the present century revolt against that dominance has become one of the striking features of the human scene. It is bringing emancipation from the political control of Western Europeans and is restive under the remnants of economic control. But more and more all the rest of the world is being shaped by the forces which have issued from Western Europe and from the descendants of Western Europeans in the new nations which have arisen from their migrations. Among these forces are science, industrialization, nationalism, socialism, Communism, democracy, and their accompanying institutions as they are known in Western Europe, America, and Australasia. Inevitably that revolutionary dynamism has profoundly affected Europe. It is the changes wrought by it which have made Europe a "new world." They challenge Christianity to adjust itself to them.

Before we sketch these changes and seek to discover the response of Christianity and to Christianity we do well to outline that Europe which was the "old world" and the place in it held by Christianity. We can take the time to do this only in the briefest summary. However, that background is necessary if we are to understand the Europe of today and the adjustments to it which are being made by Christianity.

As we attempt to look back on it, that "old world" of Europe is seen to have had several outstanding characteristics. One was internal division within a cultural whole. Geographically Europe is a peninsula. It is the westward extension of the continent of Eurasia, with the Caspian, Black, and Mediterranean Seas on the south and oceans on the west and north. But, small though it is when compared with the other major land masses which share with it the designation of continent, it has never been united politically. Indeed, Western and Central Europe have been marked by a fragmentation which has made for marked cultural variation within the inclusive whole. That inclusive cultural whole was derived largely from Greece and Rome.

In the main the Christian Church was the vehicle by which

the Græco-Roman heritage was transmitted. In that transmission Christianity modified what was handed on, in some aspects profoundly. In the course of the centuries other alterations were made by the peoples themselves.

In the eighteenth century and well into the nineteenth much of that old Europe persisted. Indeed, important survivals are still to be found.

Christianity was an integral part of that "old world" of Europe. Thanks to the labours of thousands across the centuries, by the eighteenth century all but small minorities were professedly Christian. Enclaves holding to the Jewish faith were widely scattered. In the east, where European Russia shaded off into the heartland of Eurasia there were thousands of pagans, among them Buddhists and animists. In the southeast, mainly in the Balkans, a few million Moslems were to be found, largely deposits from the Turkish tide of invasion a few centuries earlier. But the vast majority of Europeans called themselves Christian. European civilization was regarded as Christian. Except for the portion of the empire of the Ottoman Turks which stretched into Europe, all the governments were thought of as Christian, and normally their monarchs were crowned with rites in which the obligation to rule as a Christian was formally assumed. State and Church were closely associated. In theory the two were the religious and civil wings of one social structure. In general, by 1700, the Church was subordinate and for some purposes was an arm of the state. To be sure, the Papacy still attempted to exercise control over the Roman Catholic Church and was a centre of doctrinal unity. However, in practice its administrative authority was being progressively limited and, notably in France, Spain, and Portugal and later in Austria, there were national churches which to a greater or less extent were controlled by the state. The Orthodox Churches of Eastern Europe were subject to the state. In Russia that state was ostensibly Christian. In the Turkish realms it was Moslem.

The Christianity of Europe was varied. In general it was divided among three wings of the faith—Roman Catholic, Orthodox, and Protestant. In spite of its control by the state in some countries, in the main the Roman Catholic Church displayed a large degree of unity. Its monastic orders, its congregations, its theology, much of its ritual, and many of its customs over-passed political boundaries. Its use of Latin and its doctrinal allegiance to the Popes served to bind it together. The Orthodox Churches had no structural unity compared with that of the Roman Catholic Church, but they boasted a strong sense of family unity. By its genius, Protestantism was much more divided than were the other two major wings of the Christian Church. Its subjection to the state enhanced its divisions. Yet among many of its leaders there was a consciousness of a common heritage and a tie through Christ and the Scriptures.

Forces, some of them in part from Christianity, have profoundly modified the "old world" of Europe. Several of the changes have been radical. They have been mounting since the beginning of the eighteenth century, or even earlier. In the present century they have reached their largest proportions. They are still in progress, with even more drastic ones in the offing.

The main aspects of these changes are familiar to all students of recent history and to those who know the present scene. One of them has been the march of science, with the development of the scientific method and the phenomenal expansion of the knowledge of man's physical environment. Closely related to science is man's increased mastery of his physical environment. This is seen in the machine age with the industrial revolution, the rise and spread of factories, and

the improved means of transportation and communication
through the steamship, the railway, the electric tram, the auto-
mobile, the airplane, the electric telegraph, the telephone,
radio, and television. It is also seen in the moving pictures.
Intimately connected with these last two changes has been
what is sometimes known as "modern mass society." It is
prominent in the development of urban life, with cities larger
than mankind has ever known. It is notable in the particular
form of social organization and the routine which have grown
up in connexion with factories and mines. Cities are not new,
but their present dimensions would not have been possible but
for the machines. The machines tend to depersonalize those
who operate them and to make of them human cogs, repeating
endlessly the same operation. As a rule, the cities are singularly
lacking in a sense of community. They, too, are depersonal-
ized and are more and more atomized, composed of individuals with but little if any sense of belonging to others in the
same neighbourhood. With the factories, mines, and means of
transportation there has arisen a self-conscious class usually
called labour. "Labour" has been more and more organized
into unions for mutual protection and for joint action in ob-
taining better working conditions, higher wages, and security.
Populations have mounted, notably in the cities. An ever
smaller percentage is in agriculture and the proportion of the
population in cities increases. It may be that the industrialization and urbanization of society account in large part for
two other sets of changes—the breakdown of inherited standards of morality and the weakening of the family. Associated
with earlier stages of the industrial revolution was a striking
impetus to the growth of an urban middle class. Latterly, however, the power of that class, the bourgeoisie, has been either
weakened or shattered.

Parallel with these changes and closely intertwined with

them are ideologies which have worked political revolutions. The absolute monarchies of two centuries ago have disappeared. Many ancient ruling families have been swept into the dust bin. A few survive but with greatly curtailed powers. Democracies of various kinds have taken their place. Some of these democracies are in countries of Anglo-Saxon tradition. Others, as in France, Germany, and Italy, have been influenced by that tradition but differ from it in many important respects. Still others, with the U.S.S.R. as their model and often their master, claim the name of democracy but are in stark contrast with what among Western European peoples in Europe, the Americas, and Australasia has long borne that designation. Associated with the spread of democracy have been various forms of socialism. The most extreme of these is Communism. In one form or another socialism has been adopted by all European governments. Governments have become increasingly powerful. This trend has largely gone hand in hand with the spread of socialism and the growing place of organized labour. Yet it is not identified with them. Modern means of transportation and communication have made it possible for governments to bring more and more of the life of their citizens under their control. They are called upon to assume additional responsibilities and functions. They tend to be totalitarian in the sense of directing all aspects of life. The power of the government is enhanced by nationalism. With the growth of democracy an entire population becomes self-conscious and identifies its interest with that of the state.

These many changes have intensified wars. The wars of the present century have dealt severe blows to Europe. They have been briefer than many of the major conflicts from which Europe has suffered in earlier days. Yet the two world wars of the present century have centred in Europe and in proportion to their length have been more widely destructive than any which were before them. This has been made possible by the machine age, with its mechanical means of destruction and its facilities for assembling, equipping, and sustaining huge armies, and its bringing together in the struggle the resources of a nation, including the conscription in the war effort of all but children and the aged, whether as civilians or under arms. Those forces which have made possible a totalitarian state have also made possible total war.

The wars of the twentieth century have been followed by a profound pessimism in much of Western Europe. With notable exceptions, in the nineteenth century the atmosphere of Western Europe had been optimistic. Rising wealth, imperial expansion, and political and social reforms seemed to the majority to be an evidence and guarantee of progress. Now the weakness brought by war and the fact that as an aftermath of the second global struggle Western Europe has been caught between the two hostile colossi, the U.S.S.R. and the United States, have appeared to many to presage further and possibly final destruction.

In spite of augmented nationalism progress has been made in international organizations which have embraced most of Europe. Such was the League of Nations, with its headquarters in Europe. Now there is the United Nations. There are also such bodies as the Postal Union and the International Red Cross. There is, too, the movement which is bringing together much of Western Europe for economic coöperation and common defense. Similar efforts are multiplying.

It is significant that most of the movements and forces which have made Europe the "new world," except those mentioned in the last paragraph, have worked against Christianity. The emphasis upon the sufficiency of human reason which has found expression, among other channels, in the scientific advance, has appeared to leave no room for the action of God in revelation. Some of the findings of science have been interpreted as disclosing that the Scriptures are untrustworthy, notably in their account of creation and in their reports of miracles. Many honest, intelligent souls have been perplexed. Some have fully abandoned the Christian faith. Others have become agnostics, a term coined in the nineteenth century to describe a conviction that the evidence is insufficient either to affirm or to deny the tenets of Christianity. "Modern mass society" has tended to weaken or erase the Christian heritage among those who are caught up in it, partly because the routine of life in factory and mine has made difficult attendance at church services and to some degree because of the deadening effect of being a part of a machine and of association with others in the kind of routine to which the Christian faith seems irrelevant or hostile. In the cities churches have found difficulty in keeping pace with the growth and the changing character of urban life. This has been due to the necessity of building new structures and, even more, of adjusting to the new environment the kind of ministry which has been adapted to parishes in rural communities and small towns. At first the upper and middle classes were less alienated than was "labour," and although many from these classes were adversely affected by the intellectual currents, the Church outwardly maintained its hold upon them and in places for a time strengthened it. Here has been one of the factors which has caused much of "labour" and many socialists, including especially Communists, to view the churches with suspicious or hostile eye as a bulwark of an order through which they have been exploited. Partly because the Church had been successful in adjusting itself to earlier changes and thus had become a seemingly integral part of the old order, numbers of political and social liberals and radicals looked upon it as an enemy to the alterations upon which they were intent. This antagonism

has been reinforced by the hostility of several of the nineteenth-
and twentieth-century Popes to the programmes advocated by
the liberals and by the opposition of some of the other spokesmen for the churches, whether Roman Catholic, Orthodox, or
Protestant. Obviously wars entail the denial, weakening, and
for many individuals and groups destruction of moral and
spiritual values which are integral to the Christian faith.
These, as we have seen, have attained unprecedented proportions. The two world wars of the twentieth century, both in-
volving all Europe and altering even those nations which
remained neutral, have wrought incalculable damage and
have been the prelude to sweeping political and social revolutions. Most of the regimes established by the revolutions have
been either openly hostile to Christianity, as in Communist-
dominated lands, or actually if not so avowedly antagonistic.
In other words, the "new world" of Europe is adverse to
Christianity. Christianity seems to be identified with the "old
world" which is passing.

In that "new world" of Europe numerically Christianity
has been losing ground. In Russia the Bolshevik regime
brought an early disestablishment of the Orthodox Church.
With it not only was that Church deprived of state support,
of functions which it had performed for the state, of the use
of much of its property, and of a place in education, but also
the government, while professing tolerance, was actually hostile. Religious instruction to youth in groups was forbidden,
many church buildings were turned to other purposes, hundreds of the clergy were killed, imprisoned, or exiled to Siberia,
the training of new clergy was made impossible, dissensions
within the Church were fostered, an organized anti-religious
movement was encouraged, and the activities of the Church
were reduced to the holding of public services. In the 1940's
and 1950's restrictions were lightened, but the Orthodox

Church was still subservient to the state—not, to be sure, through direct control, but by the endorsement by the Church of the foreign policies of the government. The numbers of church buildings, monasteries, theological seminaries, and clergy began to increase but by mid-century had not attained pre-1917 dimensions. Some churches other than the Orthodox were permitted, notably the Evangelicals and Baptists. In states within the Russian orbit, including those in the Balkans and Central Europe, the attitude of the government was also hostile, especially towards the Roman Catholic Church. The result was that in Russia and the Russian zone millions who once bore the Christian name and other millions of Christian ancestry who have come into the world since the Communist triumph have had no contact with the Church and are not even nominally Christian.

In Western Europe de-Christianization has not gone as far as in the Communist world. The large majority of the population have been baptized. In some lands the majority go beyond baptism and are confirmed. A substantial proportion use Christian rites for weddings and funerals. Thus a formal connexion is preserved with Christianity in the major events of life—birth, the transition from childhood to maturity, marriage, and death. Yet for all but a minority these have become mere social conventions. In countries where it is still required, for the majority religious instruction in the state schools does not ensure inward assent. Separation of Church and state has gone far but in few countries is it complete. In several, even some Communist areas, financial aid is given the churches by the state. In lands where Roman Catholicism prevails the separation has been by anti-clericals who have obtained control of the state. In countries where Protestantism is dominant it has often, but not always, been at the instance of churchmen who have believed association with the state to be detrimental to the Church and to compromise its true genius. In the countries where the tie between Church and state still seems strong, as in Franco Spain, the alliance has been uneasy. Indeed, it may be argued that wherever it survives the Church-state tie is a detriment to the vigorous life of the Church, that support by taxation absolves the laity from individual responsibility for the Church, that the clergy tend to become state officials to the neglect of their proper religious functions, and that the requirement of religious instruction in the state schools makes for formalism rather than deep conviction.

For millions, probably the majority, who conform to some of the outward symbols and ceremonies of the Church, there is neither intelligent appreciation of the faith nor loyalty to it. In several lands the large majority do not attend the services of the Church or take communion, even at the high festivals of Christmas and Easter. As a result, much of Western Europe must be regarded as de-Christianized. In France, for example, where de-Christianization has been in process since at least the 1790's, where disestablishment came in 1905, or nearly a half-century ago, and where Protestants number only about a million, the practising constituency of the Roman Catholic Church is said to be five or six millions, or about one in seven or eight of the population. In England and Scandinavia, where the tie between state and Church has been preserved, regular attendants and active members are probably about the same percentage as in France. It is sobering that the de-Christianization has gone farther in cities, where the forces making the "new world" have had freer course than in the rural districts, where more of the "old world" persists. Even in many rural areas the churches are weaker than they were a generation ago.

How is Christianity in Europe responding to the situation which we have summarized? If, as many believe, Christianity is dying in Europe, the prospect for it in the rest of the world may be grim. Since Europe has long been the heart of Christendom, the demise of the faith there might mean its eventual disappearance elsewhere. Although, as we are to remind ourselves more than once, Christianity is continuing its spread and is more nearly world-wide than ever before, its parlous condition in Europe may be a foreshadowing of what is to take place elsewhere as the forces which have worked against it gain momentum. Originating in Europe, they have moved out from that continent and presumably will more and more make themselves felt. Will the current continued growth of Christianity in most regions outside Europe prove to be an example of "social lag," a last gasp of a faith which is already moribund in its historic centre?

As we survey the European scene we find that Christianity is far from finished. It is a minority movement. Probably true Christians have always been a minority, but now that so many have become either avowedly non-Christian or openly indifferent, the contrast tends to be more striking. That minority is displaying much vigour. In doing so it is not only making itself felt in Europe and in other parts of the world; it is also modifying the expressions of its faith. While true to the historic Gospel, the Christianity of the Europe of the mid-twentieth century reflects the influence of its environment. In a number of significant ways it is unlike that of yesterday and is clearly adapting itself to the world of today.

One of the striking ways in which the Christianity of Western Europe of the mid-twentieth century differs from that of a generation ago is in theology. Here it reflects the pessimism and the loss of confidence in man's ability and essential goodness which are part of the climate of opinion in Western Europe. As we have noted, the Occident came to the end of the nineteenth century on a wave of optimism. The dominant note was progress. Through using his mind and his will man had seemed to be freeing himself from the ills which had been his traditional lot. The course of evolution to which the Darwinian hypothesis had accustomed him, especially as popularized for intellectuals by Herbert Spencer, had encouraged representative Western European man to believe that the course of the race is ever upward and onward. This view was reflected in the Protestant theology which is associated with the names of Ritschl and Harnack. It regarded Jesus as having come to inaugurate an ideal society as the Kingdom of God and tended to believe that by coöperating with God men could aid in the realization of that dream. To be sure, there were many Protestant Christians who did not share that conviction and who, despairing of making the world better, looked forward to the time when by cataclysmic intervention God would destroy the present order and inaugurate the new and better age. They believed this to be the teaching of the Scriptures. However, for the moment the trend was against them. Then came the two world wars with their revelation of the insecurity of civilization and of a strain in man which is worse than bestial. To many this came as a profound shock and compelled them to reconsider the nature of man and the fashion in which God works in the world. As a result there was a shift in theological emphasis, particularly in Protestantism, for that form of the faith is more responsive to environmental changes than is Roman Catholicism or Eastern Orthodoxy. The sinfulness of man was recognized afresh and with it the suffering and degradation which man brings on himself by his greatest and basic sin, pride. Among many sensitive souls the tragedy of human existence was stressed and the inability of man by his reason and his will to extricate himself from it. Emphasis was laid upon the initiative of God in revealing Himself in His action for man's salvation through the

Incarnation, the Cross, the Resurrection, and the coming of His Holy Spirit. The name which stands out most prominently is that of Karl Barth, but there were others, some of whom did not take so extreme a position and left more room for natural theology, namely, the ability of man through his reason to learn something of God. However, the trend was to stress man's sin and helplessness and the act of God, through His love and through the grace, the unearned and quite undeserved favour of God in Jesus Christ for man's redemption. In a sense this was not new. It was as old as the Gospel. Again and again it had been reaffirmed, never more notably than by Luther. Kierkegaard had put it baldly, and it is significant that he was now discovered and influenced many who found him voicing that for which they were groping. In Britain P. T. Forsyth had brought it out early in the century in writings to which many of his fellow countrymen recurred as they sought for guidance in the new day. Yet the prominence given to this conviction reflects the condition in which Western European man found himself in the age which began with World War I.

It is also significant that some of the most active Roman Catholic theological thinking has been in that very France where de-Christianization has been proceeding longest and has gone farther than in any other country where that wing of the faith has been dominant. Here the names of Maritain and Gilson stand out, but only as the chief figures in a ferment of creative revival in Christian thought. There has been sufficient vitality in the Roman Catholic Church in France not only to survive what looked like the disastrous blow of the disestablishment of 1905 but also to put forth fresh life.

Refugee Russian scholars in France have also given proof that there is vigour in the Orthodox Church. They have been a small group, but as they have wrestled with the problems with which the agony in Europe and especially in their native land has confronted them, they have produced books which have commanded attention far outside Russian Orthodox circles. Particularly stimulating and sobering are the writings of Berdyaev.

In spite of the impoverishment brought them by the two world wars of the twentieth century, out of their diminished resources the Christians of Western Europe have put forth heroic efforts to relieve the suffering which they have seen about them and to rebuild damaged or destroyed church fabrics and institutions. Thus, aided by fellow Christians in other lands, *Hilfswerk,* an organ of German Protestants, has had noteworthy accomplishments to its credit. More assistance has come to *Hilfswerk* from the United States than from any other country, but in proportion to their populations far more has been from Sweden and Switzerland, and that in spite of the fact that active Christians in these two lands are a minority. Much aid has gone to the Continent from the Christians of the British Isles. This has been in addition to the burden which they have carried in restoring their own churches which had been put out of commission by the bombings and in constructing additional ones in the new suburbs of expanding cities. In Germany the Protestant Home Building Society has to its credit several thousand new building units. In ravaged Greece the Church Rebuilding Fund raised two million dollars to put again into operation structures which had been victims of the war which followed the war. Christians have exerted themselves to care for and help rehabilitate the incredible millions of refugees whom the two wars uprooted from their old homes. The need took on much more tragic dimensions as a result of World War II than of World War I, and that when Europeans were less able to come to the rescue than at the end of the first struggle. In Germany, for example, are centres in which refugee boys are trained in useful occupations.

Some efforts have been made not only to assist in rehabilitating the victims of the ills of the social structure but also to grapple with the basic causes of those ills. As examples we remember that the Universal Christian Council for Life and Work arose largely out of the efforts of Archbishop Söderblom, Primate of the Church of Sweden. Shortly after the outbreak of World War I he sent out an appeal in an attempt to bring Christians together in behalf of peace. Eventually, through intermediate stages, in 1925 a conference convened in Stockholm from which came the continuing organization called for short "Life and Work" and which sought to bring Christians together in efforts to create a better social, economic, political, and international world society. Later it coöperated with the World Conference on Faith and Order to bring into being the World Council of Churches, of which more in a moment.

On a national scale most of the churches of the British Isles joined in 1924 in a Conference on Christian Politics, Economics, and Citizenship, usually abbreviated as COPEC. The Iona movement, with a centre on that island from which much of the conversion of Scotland was accomplished nearly fourteen centuries ago, has given itself to the permeation with the Gospel of all of the life of that country, especially in the cities. It seeks to bring together leaders of labour, to win their confidence when, as is usual, they are alienated from Christianity, and to stimulate them to think through their problems in industry in the light of the Gospel. It endeavours to encourage the rank and file of labour to take more responsibility in their unions and other organizations. On Iona labour and clergy come together for worship and for work on some of the buildings. To help solve the problems of the industrial age the Church of Scotland has initiated the Scottish Christian Industrial Order.

In the Netherlands the Reformed Church in the Kerk en

Wereld Institute trains young men and women to reach the unchurched, largely through social service. At Sigtuna, near Stockholm, is a centre which has as its object drawing into a thoroughly Christian atmosphere for longer or shorter periods groups from various walks of life. It is largely an attempt to reach the de-Christianized intellectuals.

In Germany after World War II what are called Evangelical Academies have multiplied. They have as their purpose helping members of various occupations and professions to think through the meaning of the Christian faith for them in their daily lives and seeking to make of each a calling with distinctively Christian standards. They endeavour to stimulate the formation of groups of Christian labourers in factories with the object of bearing Christian witness not only to individuals but also in the collective life of the plant. They strive to inspire and train lay people for more active participation in the work of the local parish in a land where by tradition the laity have tended to act as though that was the responsibility of the clergy with themselves as passive beneficiaries. Haus Friedenwald, a post-World War II undertaking in Germany, concentrates on bringing the Gospel to bear on organized labour, now so largely alienated from the churches.

In Finland is the Laymen's Institute, which seeks to do for that land what Sigtuna is doing for Sweden and what the Evangelical Academies are accomplishing in Germany. We must also remark the *Zoe* or *Life* movement in the Orthodox Church in Greece. Arising around the turn of the century from the impulse brought by a great preacher, it has brought fresh vigour into that ancient body. From it has sprung a celibate brotherhood which leads a devoted communal life that has fostered hundreds of Sunday Schools and through them has brought religious nurture to thousands of children. It has trained leadership for the churches and stimulated the production of an extensive literature for popular consumption.

Likewise of significance is the growth of the Liturgical Movement in the Roman Catholic Church. It has as its aim the revival of congregational life by making it possible for the laity to participate intelligently and vocally in the Eucharist, as it did in the Early Church.

On the international scale we must note work camps which bring together in Christian fellowship in labour and worship youths from various countries. In that general area we call to mind the Churches Commission on International Affairs in which the World Council of Churches and the International Missionary Council join. While arising from American initiative, it was organized at a meeting in Cambridge after World War II and has had much of its leadership from Britain and the Continent.

These examples by no means exhaust the list of movements in Western Europe which from one or another angle have been seeking to bring all of life to a recognition of Christian standards and to approach approximation to them. They reflect the response of Western European Christianity to its changing environment and the efforts so to conform to it as to transform it.

In somewhat similar fashion European Christians have not been content with permitting their lands to be captured by forces hostile or indifferent to their faith but have reached out to the de-Christianized in efforts, some of them novel, so to present the Gospel to them as to win them to it. Here again there has been and is great variety. In France there have been CIMADE teams (CIMADE standing for *Comité Inter-Mouvements Auprès des Evacués*). They originated during the German invasion in World War II as attempts to make contact with youths from the scattered parishes and so to preserve something of church life. They also helped with refugees from the Allied invasion in the later stage of the war and in camps for political refugees. Several French Protestant movements have sprung up to reach the unevangelized. Also in France have been Roman Catholic priests trained to work in lay garb side by side with the labourers, who have long been de-Christianized, and by intimately sharing their life to win them to the faith. Because some of them tended to identify themselves so fully with labour as to be accused of extreme radicalism and even of sympathy with the Communism which is strong in that stratum of the population, in 1953 Rome took restrictive measures. However, the method has powerful advocates among the French hierarchy.

In Britain there have been industrial chaplains, many of them in the munitions factories during World War II and some in various factories after the guns became silent. In England, too, the Methodists have had what are called Commando campaigns to win those out of touch with the churches. In London after World War II the Anglicans organized a city-wide mission to bring the Gospel to the unchurched, and a similar effort was made in at least one diocese in another part of the country. The purpose of "Tell Scotland" of the mid-1950's has been the enlistment of the laity and clergy to reach those who have been out of intimate touch with the Gospel.

Germany has been the scene of several kinds of programmes for approaching those who have been all but lost to the Church. Partly for this purpose and partly to inspire the loyal laity has been the *Kirchentag*. This has brought together annually from the entire country great throngs to some large city to hear preaching and thus to contribute to a spiritual rebirth of the nation. The Gossner Mission has added to its enterprises in the non-Occident an effort to win the de-Christianized labourers of Germany. In Denmark and Norway the Inner

Mission has long been training laymen for evangelism among the masses.

As one looks back over the record of these many efforts he is aware that no large numbers of the de-Christianized have been reclaimed: there has been no mass movement back to the churches. Yet here are examples of the response of Christians to the new Europe and therefore of modifications in the Christianity of that region. What are sometimes called "creative minorities" are emerging, unmistakable evidence of vigour.

One of the most frequently told stories of the present century has been the varying responses of Christians and the churches to the totalitarian regimes of the "new world" of Europe. We recall the German Christians, as they were called, who sought to bring Protestants together in a nation-wide organization which would parallel the National Socialist state of Hitler and coöperate with it. We remember the protests which arose against it and other Nazi measures and which took form in the Confessional Church. It is significant that from this Confessional Church has come much of the leadership of the Protestant churches in Germany since World War II. We remind ourselves of the part that churchmen had in resisting the Nazi overlords in the Netherlands, Denmark, and Norway. We note the strain between the Catholic Church in Italy and the Fascist government and the eventual accommodation of the two to each other with the creation of the Vatican State, its recognition by Mussolini, the assent of the Papacy to the existence of the Fascist regime, and other concessions on both sides. We are aware of the uneasy alliance of the Roman Catholic Church in Spain with Franco and the *Falange*.

We are even more cognizant of the reciprocal hostility of the Roman Catholic Church and Communism. Here are two rival totalitarianisms, neither of which can work with the other without surrender. Each has marshaled its forces against the other. Both have suffered. In the main the Roman Catholic Church has lost more than has Communism. In Russia its numbers have dwindled. In Central Europe most of the Uniates who more than three centuries earlier came over to Rome from Orthodoxy, now, under pressure or at least encouragement from the Communists, have left Rome and rejoined the Orthodox family. In Poland, Hungary, and Czechoslovakia the Roman Catholic Church has been hard pressed. On the other side, in the early post-World War II elections in Italy the Roman Catholic Church threw its vast weight against Communism and the latter lost when the scales seemed to be tipping in its favour.

We have already remarked the accommodation of the Russian Orthodox Church to the Communist Kremlin and the measure of toleration gained by its acquiescence and support. In the Communist-dominated Balkan countries, in a somewhat similar manner, the Orthodox Churches have been forced to come to heel but have been permitted to continue their ritualistic functions.

In Latvia and Estonia the record of Protestantism is grim, and the restrictions on the Protestants in Hungary and Eastern Germany are so well known as not to need repetition. In East Germany particularly the Church has been under the cross and with a record of heroic resistance. In Czechoslovakia the Protestant minority appears to have acquiesced to the Communist regime as the wave of the future.

Here again Christianity has become different from what it was before the appearance of the totalitarian regimes. But in the main it has held to its distinctive core.

A striking feature of the response of Christianity to the new Europe has been the fashion in which Christians have been coming together in fellowships which transcend historic confessional and denominational boundaries. These are by no means all-inclusive. They are not confined to Europe nor have all of them sprung from that continent. Nor can they be ascribed solely to a deliberate adaptation to their environment. They have arisen in large part from that phase of the inner core of the faith which has as its dream the unity in love of all who bear the name of Christ. They recall the parting command of Christ to his disciples that they love one another and have as a continuing inspiration the prayer that all those who believe in Christ should be one, even as the Father is in the Son and the Son in the Father.

The Roman Catholic Church has officially stood aloof from all efforts for unity which do not acknowledge the Papacy as the divinely appointed means to that end. In that church the trend toward absolute control by the Pope which gained headway in the nineteenth century has continued. This was made vivid by the Papal initiative in declaring (1950) that the bodily assumption to heaven of the Virgin Mary is to be believed by all the faithful. The first solemn definition of dogma since, in 1854, the Pope came out for the immaculate conception of the Virgin and since the Vatican Council of 1870 endorsed Papal infallibility, it met with far less criticism from within the church than did the latter action. It was thus evidence of the heightened power of the Pope within that communion. More and more the Roman Catholic Church is a tightly knit world-wide organization directed from the Vatican, a self-conscious minority in a hostile world which it is seeking to win to its form of the faith.

More inclusive is a trend with Protestant leadership. It began in the nineteenth century and in the twentieth century it has been gaining momentum. It takes many forms but is conscious that all these are expressions of one "Ecumenical Movement," namely, one that aspires to be as comprehensive as all mankind and which dreams of bringing together all Christians. One group of manifestations is fellowships of Christians who come into them as individuals and not as churches. Outstanding among these are the Young Men's and Young Women's Christian Associations. Each has its world headquarters in Geneva. Both have drawn into membership not only individuals of many Protestant denominations but also thousands of Roman Catholics and Orthodox. For instance, in Poland, before the days when they were banned by the Communist regime, the membership of the Young Men's Christian Associations was overwhelmingly Roman Catholic. In Greece it is Orthodox. Yet the World's Alliance of the Young Men's Christian Association which is made up of the various national movements is predominantly Protestant. So, too, is the World's Committee of the same brotherhood. Mostly American in its leadership, with far more members in the United States than in any other country, and drawing its financial support mainly from the United States, the World's Committee has much of its personnel in Europe. Similar is the World's Student Christian Federation. It began largely at the instance of Americans and its first and long-time chief executive was an American, John R. Mott. But its headquarters are also in Geneva, much of its membership is in Europe, and it, too, cuts across confessional lines and in its constituency has Orthodox and Roman Catholics as well as Protestants. The Evangelical Alliance, which as a means of bringing Protestants together had its heyday in the nineteenth century but still exists, originated in Europe. Philip Schaff, its chief promoter in the United States, was European born and educated. The World Council of Christian Education, formerly the World's Sunday School Association, has been overwhelmingly British and American in membership and leadership. The Sunday Schools began in

England, the first of the World's Sunday School Conventions convened in London, and the one in which the World's Sunday School Association was organized met in Rome.

The two chief ecumenical bodies are the International Missionary Council and the World Council of Churches. While the former was constituted in a meeting in the United States and all its chairmen have been from that country, it came out of the World Missionary Conference held in Edinburgh in 1910 and it was a German, Gustav Warneck, who first suggested the main features of such an organization. Composed of national councils, conferences, and committees, it has members on all five continents and in Australasia and brings together in coöperation representatives of the large majority of Protestants. The World Council of Churches is even more inclusive. As its name indicates, its members are churches, including not only those having the large majority of the Protestants of the world but also the Greek Orthodox Church and several Old Catholic Churches. It was organized in Europe, its headquarters are in Geneva, and the majority of its presidents and secretaries have been Europeans. In contrast with the United States, where several of the larger Protestant bodies have held aloof, in Europe all the major Protestant churches are members and the member churches comprise the overwhelming majority of the Protestants of that area.

In addition to these global organizations, the Protestants of Europe are coming together in coöperation on a national and regional scale. Thus the British Council of Churches, organized in 1942, includes all the larger and several of the smaller Protestant church bodies of the British Isles, while its counterpart in the United States, although embracing the majority of Protestants and some non-Protestant churches, has not been able to attract several of the major Protestant church bodies in that country. After World War II all but one of the regional bodies of Germany, the *Landeskirchen,* came together in a loose federation, EKID, the Evangelical Church in Germany, thus continuing a process which had begun between the two world wars. There has been talk of a larger association of the Protestant churches of all Europe.

As, then, we survey the Christianity of Europe and its response to the movements which have made of that continent "the new world," we note that it is displaying marked vitality and in so doing is in part conforming to that world but without surrendering the continuing and essential core of the faith. While in Western Europe the large majority of the population still hold superficially to the earlier tradition and are baptized and present their children for baptism, those who maintain an active connexion with the Church are a minority. For the majority de-Christianization has proceeded far. Yet issuing from that minority are fresh formulations of the Christian faith which emphasize its essential features, efforts to relieve the suffering attendant upon the agony through which the continent has been passing, movements to attack the basic manifestations of that agony, a variety of approaches to the de-Christianized, mostly new and designed to meet the current conditions, and progress among both Roman Catholics and Protestants, particularly among the latter, in facing the world unitedly, not in self-defense but to witness to the Gospel.

CHAPTER III

The Distinctive Features of the Christianity of the United States

How has Christianity responded to the conditions which it faces in the United States? In what ways has it been modified by factors peculiar to that country? In Europe we often hear the statement that in the United States Christianity is being compromised by what is called Americanism. At one time that charge aroused apprehension in some Roman Catholic circles on the Continent and brought about a Papal warning to the outstanding member of the hierarchy in the United States. It has been more frequent in Protestant circles.

It is a temptation to extend the inquiry beyond the United States to the other nations, mostly in America, which have arisen from emigration from Europe. Canada presents a unique picture, by no means identical with that of the other countries in the Western Hemisphere. There Protestantism, overwhelmingly Anglo-Saxon and coöperating through the Canadian Council of Churches, is paralleled by a strong Roman Catholic community, predominantly French and a symbol and bond of French nationalism but unsympathetic with France. The Roman Catholic community also contains an uncongenial Irish minority. Latin America, as we have suggested, is often regarded as Roman Catholic, and in most of the republics that church has a privileged official status. However, in contrast with its vigour in French Canada, in Latin America the Roman Catholic Church has lost the real allegiance of many of the intellectuals, does not produce enough clergy to supply its needs but depends upon Europe and the United States to make up the deficiency, and makes almost no contribution of personnel to foreign missions. In other words, Latin-American Catholicism, although more than four centuries old, is a liability to its communion rather than an asset. By contrast, Protestantism is rapidly growing. It has not sprung from the soil but has been introduced from Europe and the United States. But increasingly, notably in the largest of the Latin-American republics, Brazil, it is taking root and is spreading through the initiative of the native-born. Moreover, Latin-American Protestantism tends to be very conservative theologically, and in Chile the largest denomination is the Pentecostals, one which in the United States, although active, is a small minority.

It is also with reluctance that we dismiss with a sentence or two the Christianity of Australasia—Australia and New Zealand. In each land it has responded to its environment. While mostly from the British Isles, transplanted into its new habitat it both reproduces what it brought with it and has been modified, partly in the proportionate numerical strength of the various churches, partly in the altered status of the Church of England and the separation of Church and state, and partly in the temper of each of the two Dominions.

However, among those nations which have arisen from the migrations of Europeans we must direct our primary attention to the United States. That, as we said earlier, is because of the prominence of that country in the current world scene and the corresponding place which its churches have in present-day

Christianity. Far more Protestant missionaries go from the United States than from any other one land, the number of Roman Catholic missionaries from the United States is rapidly mounting, more than half the funds to support the various Protestant international organizations are from the United States, the Vatican is said to be increasingly dependent financially on the Roman Catholics of the United States, the scholarship of Protestants of the United States in theological and Biblical subjects is being viewed with growing respect in Europe as well as in the younger churches in Asia and Africa founded by missions, each year more students from other countries are enrolled in the theological schools of the United States, and church methods worked out in that country are having increasing influence upon those of the churches in other lands.

What are the features of the history and life of the United States in response to which its Christianity has developed distinctive characteristics? To a large extent the culture of the United States is a geographic extension of that of Europe. Intellectual and social movements and political events in Europe have had and continue to have repercussions in the United States. Yet the United States has long ceased to be either culturally or politically a colony of Europe. The currents coming from east of the Atlantic mingle in a fashion different from that in the lands of their origin and to them are added currents issuing from springs in the United States. The American environment is not a reproduction of that of Europe.

Here is not the place to enter upon an extended description of the United States and its culture. We must, however, outline such of the outstanding distinctive marks as affect the religious scene.

The United States began as British colonies. From the British Isles came most of the settlers of the colonial period. They brought with them the English language, English customs, and English institutions. These have continued, with important modifications. In the founding of several of the early colonies the religious motive was strong. In none was it the only one, but it was prominent in the four New England colonies and in Pennsylvania and Georgia, and it was present in at least two others. However, the large majority of the settlers came to better their economic lot. This meant that in the new environment only a small minority of them and their children took the trouble to become members of churches. They were from lands where there were state churches, where, except for Jews, baptism was universal, and where, in one form or another, churches were community institutions and were maintained by endowments or public taxation or both. While in most of the Thirteen Colonies a connexion between Church and state existed, for the most part it was much weaker than in the Europe of that day. De-Christianization was a real danger. Indeed, for many thousands, perhaps the majority, it was more than a danger: it was taking place. This was not so much by open denial as by neglect and absorption in other concerns.

After independence the danger of de-Christianization was enhanced. By its constitution the Congress of the new national government was forbidden to make any "law respecting an establishment of religion or prohibiting the free exercise thereof." In several of the individual states full religious liberty was soon enacted, and the nineteenth century was still young when (1833) the last trace of support of the churches through public taxation was abolished. As immigration poured in during the nineteenth and twentieth centuries and as westward migration from the older states mounted, the menace of de-Christianization continued. Indeed, it is still present, perhaps never more so. Not only does the movement to the West persist, but also through most of the country population seems to be increasingly shifting—from rural districts to cities, from one city to another, and from one section of a city to another section. Hundreds of thousands are chronically migrant and do not put down roots in any community. The intellectual factors which in Europe have contributed to de-Christianization also operate. So do the various aspects of "modern mass society" which we have noted in Europe. Among these are the growth of cities, with the atomization of their inhabitants and lack of community, and conditions in factories and mines which are a challenge to Christian morals, absorb labourers in the latters' own organizations, and make seemingly irrelevant, difficult, or impossible participation in traditional church life.

We must also take into account the religious heritage of the United States when, in the latter part of the eighteenth century, the new nation achieved its political independence.

That heritage was predominantly Protestant. Roman Catholics were a small minority. Protestantism was varied. It was chiefly from the British Isles, but in it were contingents from the Continent. The latter were mainly from the Netherlands, Germany, and Sweden. In Protestantism strains which in Europe were under legal or social disabilities, sometimes to the extent of persecution, were proportionately much more prominent than in the mother lands. What in Europe were state churches were represented—the Church of England, Lutheranism, Reformed, both Dutch and German, and Presbyterianism. However, the Scotch-Irish immigration in the eighteenth century, from which much of American Presbyterianism sprang, was from the North of Ireland seeking refuge from unhappy economic conditions and from a land where the established church was Anglican. In New England the dominant form of Protestantism was the later Congregationalism, made up of a fusion of Puritans and Independents. Quakers and Baptists were prominent in religiously tolerant Rhode Island, sharing that colony with other groups, among whom Congregationalists were important. In Pennsylvania, founded by one of their number, Quakers were a minority, but they were influential, and the colony became a haven for several of the small, persecuted radical Protestant groups from the Continent.

It is sometimes said that the Protestantism of the Thirteen Colonies was prevailingly Puritan. If by Puritan is meant what the term designated in England, the generalization is misleading. In that sense, Puritan elements were strong in New England and here and there in some of the other colonies, notably in parts of New York and New Jersey, but elsewhere they were either weak or entirely absent. However, the Reformed branch of Protestantism, of which Puritans were an offshoot, was much more widely spread, for in it must also be included the Dutch and some of the German settlers, the Presbyterians, and the Baptists.

Moreover, what may loosely be called Pietism was potent in much of the colonial Protestantism. Like Puritanism, that designation is not entirely accurate. Strictly speaking, it describes a particular German movement which stressed the experience of commitment and conversion. It was early represented in America in Muhlenberg, who, coming from its main German centre, Halle, was the outstanding pioneer in furthering and organizing Lutheranism. However, if by Pietism is meant a strain in Protestantism which emphasizes the conscious and striking conversion of the individual, it can be said to have been very widespread. It characterized the New England churches and it was the outstanding and distinctive feature of the Great Awakening which beginning in the 1720's swept through the colonies and was important in their religious life until the agitation culminating in the Revolution and separation from the mother country diverted men's attention to politics.

Characteristic of the United States has been an amazing growth in population, wealth, and physical well-being. Accompanying this have been intense activity and a contagious optimism. Men have been engaged in conquering the frontier and in developing the apparently limitless natural resources of field, forest, and mine. They have tended to believe in progress and that nothing is impossible. Acutely conscious of building a new nation and of an experiment in democracy on a colossal scale, they have looked upon Europe as the "old world" and have believed that, emancipated from its evils, they have been making a fresh start in what the Great Seal of the United States declares to be a "new order of the ages." They have, accordingly, wished to hold aloof from Europe.

Latterly Americans have found that isolation is impossible. Reluctantly and late they were drawn into the two world wars of the twentieth century. Against their will they have become engaged in the struggle with aggressive Communism and, with their wealth and physical power, in that conflict have become the leaders of the free world. Now fully in the current of world affairs, sobered and at times bewildered and impatient with the responsibilities thrust upon them, the people of the United States have wavered in their optimism. The great depression which began in 1929 reinforced that uncertainty. Fear of the future and a sense of insecurity have crept in. While by no means as pessimistic as Western Europeans, they are not as confident as formerly.

We must also note the multiplicity of racial and national elements which have entered into the population. There are the widely scattered but numerically inconsiderable American Indians. There are the European strains which date from colonial days—chiefly English, Scotch-Irish, Dutch, and German, with a sprinkling of Scots, Swedes, French Huguenots, and Jews. There are the Negroes, mostly descended from slaves brought over in the colonial period and in the first few years of independence. Then there are the offspring of the millions who, attracted by the economic opportunities in the burgeoning nation, poured in during the nineteenth and the first few years of the twentieth century. In the immigration of the first half of the nineteenth century Irish and Germans predominated. Slightly later Swedes, Norwegians, Danes, and Finns were prominent. In the latter part of the century and until World War I outstanding contributions were Italians, Poles, Hungarians, Greeks, and others from Southern, Central, and Eastern Europe and the Balkans. Jews arrived from various countries. By the mid-twentieth century more of them were there than in all the rest of the world. To the west coast came Chinese, Japanese, and a few small contingents from other countries in South and East Asia: they would have been more numerous had it not been for restrictive legislation. World War I brought a subsidence of the flood of immigration and when peace was won Congress raised barriers which kept it from attaining its former dimensions. In that immigration is much of the clue to the distinctive features of the Christianity of the United States.

As one seeks to view comprehensively the Christianity of the United States he is impressed with the fact that it is different from that in any other land and yet that in the main, in each of its many manifestations, its adherents have striven to hold to what they regard as the essential core of the faith or to return to it when they believe that it has been compromised. In one way or another the features peculiar to the Christianity of the United States reflect the history and the environment. Some are conscious adaptations, deliberate response to conditions in that country. More have arisen, almost inevitably, from other than religious factors in the history and life of the nation.

A feature which immediately stands out in the Christianity of the United States is the very great variety. More kinds of Christianity are seen than in any other country in either the past or the present, chiefly because of the many ethnic and national sources of the immigration from which the population has come. It is to imported denominations that the large majority of those who have church membership belong. Almost all, and possibly all, Christian communions and national churches which exist anywhere in the world are represented, the large majority by organized groups. The Roman Catholic Church, the various national units of the family of Orthodox Churches, several of the Eastern Churches, among them Armenians and Nestorians, and the many Protestant churches of Europe are there.

Yet, as a second distinguishing feature, most of the imported denominations have been altered by their new environment. Their temper, their proportionate strength, their relations with one another, and in some instances their theological outlook differ markedly from what had characterized them in the lands from which they came.

In the third place, to the denominations of foreign origin have been added a number which have sprung up in the United States itself. These are also varied, but they have common characteristics which reflect the American environment.

We must speak at some length about the imported denominations and the alterations which they have experienced in this new environment.

First we must note that in Europe numbers of them were state churches with the prestige and the handicaps which accrued from that position. From the prestige came a tendency to be aristocratic, to support the order of society under which they had gained power, and to view with disdain or dislike other churches, for they regarded them as schismatic heresies and as threats to true religion and to the unity of the nation. Among the handicaps were dependence upon taxation rather than voluntary offerings of the members and in some countries the attitude of a large proportion of the laity, which looked upon baptism and confirmation simply as social conventions entailed by being citizens, regarded the clergy as civil officials, and, except for a small minority of devoted spirits, left to the clergy the running of the churches and even, notably but not exclusively in Roman Catholic lands, viewed the Church and the clergy with hostile eye.

In the United States, in contrast, as we have seen, no one church is established by law, support to the churches from public funds has not been given (except in some periods to missions to the Indians, and here on the ground that they were civilizing rather than religious agencies and then without discrimination between denominations), full religious liberty is a legal principle, and in theory no official priority is accorded to any church.

To be sure, the state is not irreligious nor is there complete separation of Church and state. The large majority of the state constitutions in their preambles give recognition to God. The Supreme Court has said in so many words that "we are a Christian people." In some states, courts have declared Christianity to be part of the common law. Christian ethics are generally accepted as standard. Coins bear the declaration "In God we trust." The officially adopted national anthem, "The Star-Spangled Banner," has a verse which recognizes Divine providence. The President takes his oath of office on the open Bible. Each house of Congress has a Christian chaplain. In the armed services chaplains—Protestants, Roman Catholic, and Jewish—are appointed with the rank, status, and pay of officers. Annually a day for national thanksgiving is set apart by presidential proclamation.

When churches from abroad were transplanted to the American scene, they underwent striking changes in position and in relation to one another. If they were to take root and persist it would have to be by voluntary contributions of money. At the outset, some of these came from Europe. However, the main and eventually the entire burden was carried by the American constituency. From members and their friends came, and come, the funds to erect church buildings, to educate and support clergy, and to aid in the spread of the faith to other lands. To an amazing degree these ends have been accomplished. Literally billions of dollars have been poured into church structures, church schools, and the salaries of those who give their full time to the churches. Some of this money has come from the wealthy. Much has come from millions of the lower-income groups. Increasingly the principle of voluntary giving to religion has become the rule in other countries, but in no other land has it reached such large dimensions as in the United States.

Another change has been from the dignity of a state church, which was that of several of the bodies in Europe, to being one among many churches and with a decidedly lower social status than in the mother country. One reason for the success of the churches, especially but not exclusively of the nineteenth-century immigration, is that they have been identified with a particular ethnic or racial group. Often his church was the main and sometimes the only institution which the immigrant recognized as familiar and in which he had an accepted place. Here, in the midst of an English-speaking nation, he heard his own tongue in sermons and, in Protestant bodies, in hymns and liturgy. He met those of his own kind. He participated in ceremonies and forms of worship which he had known before he crossed the ocean. What in Europe was a state church, therefore, became not the church of the nation but the church of a particular ethnic community.

This has been particularly true of Protestant and Eastern churches. Norwegians, Swedes, Danes, Icelanders, Finns, and Germans have each had their own Lutheran synods. Not all of each of these nationalities have been in one synod. The Germans, being more numerous than any of the others, have had several synods, and the Norwegians were slow in coming together in a single body. Latterly the Orthodox have divided into bodies which reflect their national origins. For example, the Greek Orthodox Church has flourished because of its support by the Greeks, some of them wealthy.

For a time in the nineteenth century it looked as though the Roman Catholic Church might proliferate into several national bodies, each in communion with Rome but administratively and ethnically distinct. That trend, however, was overcome and almost all were brought structurally under one hierarchy. The major exception has been the Polish National Catholic Church of America. Here complete separation from Rome was effected, mainly over resentment against the authority which the clergy claimed over the laity.

Socially most of the churches which had privileged positions east of the Atlantic were looked down on by the older American stock. The older stock, predominantly Anglo-Saxon and English-speaking, tended to view the newer immigration with dislike and suspicion as "foreign" and hence regarded their churches with a mixture of fear and disdain as alien to the American tradition. That attitude was enhanced by the fact that most of the immigrants came as refugees from difficult, sometimes famine, conditions in their homelands, were in search of better livelihood, and were from the lower economic and social levels of the countries of their origin.

The three major exceptions to this lower social status of the state churches have been the Protestant Episcopal Church and, in some places, the Presbyterian and Congregational Churches. Since in pre-independence days the Church of England had been established in several of the colonies, and since its membership was of stock which was mostly from England and therefore had the sense of security belonging to the prosperous pre-Revolutionary Anglo-Saxon elements of the population, the Protestant Episcopal Church, representing the Anglican communion, has been accorded some of the prestige which formerly accrued to the Church of England. It has attracted many from the upper-income levels, and membership in it has been associated with social recognition. Although the majority of the Presbyterians are not of direct Scottish descent, the fact that the Church of Scotland is Presbyterian and has enjoyed a privileged position in that country seems to have been reflected in the place which the Presbyterian Church holds in many communities. In numbers of places, especially but not exclusively in the older states outside of New England, it shares with the Episcopal Church the socially and economically elite. With the Episcopalians and the Presbyterians must also be grouped the Congregationalists. While never established in England—except with some other denominations during the Commonwealth—Congregational churches had been the "standing order" in colonial New England with a close association with the state. At the time of independence they were the strongest religious group in the United States. Their westward spread was chiefly through New Englanders and they never became strong in the Southern or the Middle states. Where they are present they tend to attract those of education and of high social and economic status. The same is true of the Unitarian minority who have come out of New England Congregationalism.

As time has passed the position of what may be called the ethnic churches has been modified. That has been especially true of Protestants. Some, like the Norwegian Lutheran Church, now the Evangelical Lutheran Church of America, and the General Conference of German Baptist Churches in America, organized into the North American Baptist General Conference, have dropped their distinctive national names. More important has been their tendency to conform to the patterns of the Protestant churches longer in the United States. They develop Sunday Schools. In contrast with the Continental custom of having missionary societies independent of the ecclesiastical structure, they organize missionary societies as agencies of the church. Their hymnals include contributions from other, usually Anglo-Saxon, denominations. To hold the younger generation their services are in English rather than the mother tongue. Through marriage or because of geographic propinquity and convenience as the nearest or perhaps the only church in a particular neighborhood they begin to attract members from other ethnic and denominational backgrounds. Increasingly teachers in the theological seminaries of the national churches obtain their post-graduate training in universities not under ecclesiastical control and thus bring a wider viewpoint to prospective clergy.

A striking peculiarity of the Christianity of the United States is the great growth of denominations which in England are minorities who do not conform to the Church of England and which took root in the United States in colonial days. Of these the three largest are the Congregationalists, the Methodists, and the Baptists.

As we have reminded ourselves, at the coming of political independence, the Congregationalists were the most nearly compact of the larger groups and were probably the most numerous. Although represented in some of the other colonies, they were dominant in New England and were identified with it. It was from New England that they spread, principally around nuclei of New England settlers on the westward-moving frontier. By tradition they set high value on an educated ministry. This they have continued to do. That policy has contributed to a characteristic which we have noted: their tendency to be associated with those of upper incomes and of intellectual and social culture.

This, combined with a growing freedom in organization and thought, has made Congregationalists the most liberal of the large denominations. The extreme liberals hived off to form the Unitarians, but many liberals remained within the Congregational fellowship until a substantial proportion of the clergy and laity have a theological position which does not differ greatly from that of the early Unitarians.

However, while much of the Unitarianism which has gathered into the national fellowship of its churches has moved far from historic Christianity and has even given up a belief in God, the main body of Congregationalists have held to the central core of the Christian faith. Moreover, Congregationalists have also numbered and continue to number some who are frankly conservative. From Congregationalists came the leadership in initiating the oldest of the large foreign mission agencies of the churches of the United States, the American Board of Commissioners for Foreign Missions, and while for its first half-century strong non-Congregational elements shared in its support, that society is now dependent upon the Congregational Churches and upon the Christian Churches which some years ago joined with them in their national organizations. Then, too, the three outstanding leaders of the revivals which have characterized American religious life were Congregationalists. These were Jonathan Edwards, regarded as the chief figure in the Great Awakening in the second quarter of the eighteenth century, Charles G. Finney, from whose preaching stemmed the major revivals in the second quarter of the nineteenth century, and Dwight L. Moody, who had a world-wide and profound influence in the second half of that century.

A combination of missionary passion and belief in education made Congregationalists prominent in founding schools and colleges, most of them of very high grade. As was to be expected, several, including Harvard and Yale, are in New England. Others were planted on the frontier in pioneer days and grew as that part of the country prospered. It was Congregationalists who did more than any other religious group for the education of the Negroes after emancipation. Among others, Hampton Institute, Atlanta University, and Fisk University, through the American Missionary Association, owed their beginnings and early sustenance to Congregationalists.

From Congregationalism have come some of the movements for Christian unity. It has bred many of those who have sought to bring the Gospel to bear upon all aspects of the life of the nation and the world. In the fore part of the nineteenth century it contributed notably to the anti-slavery and temperance movements and in the latter part of the century to the "social gospel."

It may be significant that the founders of several of the more prominent religious bodies which have departed furthest from the historic core of Christianity were reared in Congregationalism. That was true of the early Unitarians. Joseph Smith, the founder of the Church of Jesus Christ of Latter-Day Saints, better known as the Mormons, was born in Vermont of old New England stock. He himself grew up in western New York apart from much direct contact with Congregationalists, but the family background had been that of Congregational New England. So, too, Brigham Young, next to Joseph Smith the chief shaper of Mormonism, was of a New England family which had moved to western New York in his childhood. Mary Morse Baker Eddy, the founder of the Church of Christ Scientist and of Christian Science, in her youth was in a Congregational church. Charles Taze Russell, who inaugurated Jehovah's Witnesses, was also reared in a Congregational church.

Why has Congregationalism been a nurturing ground for such diverse movements? The answer is not clear. Many other religious movements have arisen in America, some also departing from the historic core of Christianity. However, such of them as have attained large numerical proportions and have held firmly to that core are chiefly from Presbyterian and Baptist antecedents. Barton W. Stone and Alexander Campbell, from whom sprang the Disciples of Christ and most of the main bodies of those calling themselves simply Christians, came out of Presbyterianism. For a time Alexander Campbell was affiliated with the Baptists. William Miller, counted as the founder of the movement from which issued the Seventh-Day Adventists, had for mother a devout Baptist. It may be that the secret is to be found in the greater freedom in Congregationalism.

Although it has continued to grow, in numbers Congregationalism has not kept pace with the Methodists and Baptists. By the mid-twentieth century it is still influential, but not as much as in the nineteenth century, and it is now one of several medium-sized denominations.

Methodism, like Congregationalism of English origin, has far outstripped the latter in its dimensions. This was and is true in the British Isles. In the United States the contrast is even more striking. Here it is the second largest of the Protestant denominational families and has taken on forms distinct from those in the land of its origin. At the time of the political separation of the United States from the mother country, it had barely begun to gain a footing. Its phenomenal growth was after that event. This it owed in part to its great initial leader, Francis Asbury, for, like John Wesley, he combined single-hearted devotion with high gifts of organization and administration. Yet here was not the chief reason. As in the British Isles, Methodism appealed to the common man. Its preaching was couched in language which he could understand. It sternly urged repentance and in glowing terms set forth the grace of God in Christ and the wonder and joy of salvation to those who in faith accepted that grace. Zealously missionary, with its system of circuit riders, small local classes under experienced lay leaders, conferences under the supervision of district superintendents and bishops, culminating in a national representative conference, it combined ardent efforts to win converts with provisions for nourishing them in the faith and mobilizing them for further advances. While not neglecting the urban centres, during its early decades it had its greatest growth in rural areas and on the expanding frontier. There, among the partially de-Christianized, it made great gains. It also spread to the Negroes. It won a large following among the nineteenth-century Protestant immigration. The United Brethren and the Evangelical Association, of similar temper and structure, both of American origin, spread widely among the Germans of both the eighteenth- and the nineteenth-century immigration. True to the genius of John Wesley, in the United States Methodism placed marked emphasis upon education. It gave rise to academies, colleges, universities, and theological seminaries. Perhaps in part for this reason, in later years it has tended to appeal to what may be called the middle-class elements of the older American stock.

As the frontier stage of the nation's life has passed, Methodism has become more nearly urban than in its earlier days. Towns and cities have grown in areas where Methodism was firmly planted in the pioneer days and in them it has persevered and multiplied. Partly because of its increased emphasis upon an educated ministry, in later years it has largely lost touch with the lowest-income groups in the cities and has drawn chiefly from those of middle incomes. So far as they have been reached, the humbler elements of traditionally Protestant background have been served by denominations, some of which owe their initial inspiration to Methodism, which appeal more to the emotions.

In 1939 the majority of Methodists came together in what is officially known as the Methodist Church. At the mid-twentieth-century mark it numbered about nine million members, and is the largest single Protestant ecclesiastical body in the United States. Those of the Methodist name and tradition who remain independent of it are in several churches, three of Negro membership, numerous, but all together not a third of the size of the Methodist Church.

In structure and spirit the Methodists of the United States differ somewhat from those of the mother churches. To be sure, they are very much alike, they draw from similar social strata, and they are associated in a world organization of Methodists. Yet in England Methodism is overshadowed by the Church of England and in Scotland by the Church of Scotland. In both countries it is a dissenting and non-conforming movement. In the United States, in contrast, it is among the dominant denominations, and its bishops, both in the community as a whole and in religious circles, have more prestige because of their office than do their counterparts in Britain. The very fact that in the United States Methodism has bishops and that in British Methodism that title does not exist is indicative of a difference in temper and status.

The largest Protestant denominational family in the United
States is the Baptists. It is about 50 per cent more numerous
than the Methodists. This is the more striking since in the
British Isles, from which both denominations stem, Methodists
are between two and three times as numerous as Baptists. The
difference lies largely in the Negro constituency. Negro Baptists are about 40 per cent of the whole and are about three
times as numerous as Negro Methodists. In white membership
Baptists only slightly exceed Methodists. Baptist white membership is overwhelmingly in the South while Methodism's
main strength is in the North. In several Southern states there
are more Baptists than the total of all other denominations.

In the prominence of Negro Baptists and in the fact that
Southern white Baptists far outnumber white Baptists in all the
rest of the country lies much of the clue to the character of the
Baptist movement in the United States. It ministers to what
may be called the proletariat, white and black, of the older
American stock. Because of slavery and the competition in the
labour market by Negroes both before and after emancipation,
comparatively little of the nineteenth-century immigration
from Europe went to the Southern states. The whites are overwhelmingly of pre-Revolutionary ancestry. Baptists multiplied
through the revivals of the nineteenth and twentieth centuries.
At the outset most of their clergy were men of little or no formal education. Even more than the Methodists they spoke in
language which the rank and file could understand and put
their appeal in moral and emotional terms which reached the
partially de-Christianized who had only a smattering of education. Their appeal was effective chiefly among the English-
speaking barely literate unchurched elements among whom
there were some remnants of Protestantism. These were predominantly in the South. In the North the older American
white stock seems on the average to have had a higher level of

literacy and its humbler elements were, therefore, more responsive to the Methodists, with their greater stress on education for their clergy and their laity. Moreover, the Baptist form of organization by local autonomous churches in which in principle each member has an equal voice was congenial to the rural communities in which the large majority of Southern whites had their homes.

It was natural that as Christianity spread among the Negroes it should be through a denomination which was already strong among the white elements which in economic and educational level were closest to them. It was after emancipation that Christianity grew most rapidly among the Negroes. Negroes, now free, were intent upon shaking off all control by white men. Since, after Reconstruction days and the regaining of control of local and state governments by the whites, Negroes were for the most part disfranchised and excluded from politics, the churches were the chief institutions which they could call their own. The Baptist form of organization and the Baptist type of preaching, highly emotional, were congenial to them and Baptist churches multiplied.

Latterly, social changes are affecting the Baptists, especially of the South. With the increasing prosperity in the South, Baptists in that section are developing their colleges, universities, and theological seminaries and the educational level is rising. Both Negroes and whites are moving to the rapidly growing towns and cities. Thousands of Negroes are migrating to the North, where they are finding homes not on farms, as formerly in the South, but in the great cities. Although still behind that of the white man, the educational level of the Negroes is improving. Baptist churches are reflecting some of the changes in their constituencies. In the South the educational level of Baptist white clergy and laity is mounting. Yet it is still true that of the large Protestant denominations Baptists have the lowest economic and educational level. That is the case in both South and North and among both whites and Negroes.

In the numerical prominence of Methodists and Baptists is seen another feature of the Christianity of the United States: its spread among the de-Christianized. It may be called the conversion of the American population. Together Methodists and Baptists constitute slightly more than half of the Protestants of the United States and are almost as numerous as the Roman Catholics. Indeed, since Baptists do not baptize infants and count as members only the baptized, and Roman Catholics count infants as well as adults, Methodists and Baptists may together outnumber them. That is because Methodists and Baptists have stressed "evangelism," the winning of the unchurched. The proportion of church members in the population of the United States has mounted fairly steadily. So far as figures can be had, at the time the Thirteen Colonies became the United States church members were only about five in a hundred of the population. By 1800 the proportion had risen to about seven in a hundred, by 1850 to about fifteen in a hundred, by 1900 to about thirty-five in a hundred, and by 1950 to about fifty-seven in a hundred. The percentage is about the same among the whites, out of their European background Christian in heritage if not by profession, and among Indians and Negroes, non-Christian by ancestry. Both the de-Christianized whites and the non-Christian Indians, Negroes, and Orientals are being won to at least a formal profession of the faith. In this evangelism Methodists and Baptists have led and, accordingly, have reaped the fruits. But in it many other denominations have shared, especially those of Protestant and Anglo-Saxon lineage.

Here is another striking difference between the Christianity of the United States and that of Europe. In the latter what looks like the de-Christianization of an erstwhile professedly Christian population is taking place. In the United States conversion of the de-Christianized and the hereditarily non-Christians is in progress.

Whether the contrast is as great as figures would indicate is not certain. Statistics do not enable us to determine how much of actual Christian living has been involved in the profession of a formal church connexion either in Europe or in the United States. We do not know whether the attenuation and reduction of the church connexion in Europe means as much de-Christianization as at first appears or whether the growth in church membership in the United States has been accomplished without watering down in practice the meaning of membership. Yet the contrast is there. Although the United States is in the western European cultural tradition and many of the factors which operate in Europe are also in the United States, the environments are so far unlike that their response to Christianity and the response of Christianity to them is far from being the same.

The mounting church membership in the United States is associated with another distinctive feature of the Christianity of the country which is in response to the environment. The increase has been largely through "revivals." These, as we have suggested, have particularly characterized the older Protestant denominations of British origin. In the broadest sense of the term, namely, a fresh and contagious surge of life through the Gospel, "revivals" are not peculiar to the United States. To name only a few expressions, they have been seen in the rise of monasticism, in the recurring emergence of new monastic movements such as the Cistercians, Franciscans, Dominicans, and Jesuits, in the appearance of groups, such as the Waldensees and the Lollards, which the Roman Catholic Church regarded as heretical, in the initial rise and growth of

Protestantism, in Pietism in Germany, and in the Evangelical Awakening in England in which the Wesleys were outstanding. They were prominent in colonial America, notably in the Great Awakening. Incidentally, it is significant that they were not in all colonial America. Colonial Latin America, whether Spanish, Portuguese, or French, seems not to have had them, at least not to so marked a degree and with such ethical sequels as did the Thirteen Colonies. It was in the Thirteen Colonies that there were the first instances of what has been outstanding in the spread of much of Protestantism in the United States.

In the United States revivals have been a widely accepted means of rekindling devotion among professing Christians and of bringing to the Christian faith the de-Christianized and the non-Christians. In connexion with them techniques have been developed, some of which, at least in the emphasis given them, are peculiar to the older Protestantism of that country. Earlier and to a certain extent today they have been and are associated with gatherings, such as camp meetings and the more recent summer assemblies, in which mass suggestion has had and has a part. "Evangelistic meetings," either in an individual congregation or, often, in a city-wide "campaign" in which many congregations are mobilized, focus attention on commitment to the Christian faith. Professional itinerant "evangelists" who give their entire time to such methods are numerous. In some denominations, of the larger ones notably Methodists and Baptists, pastors of local congregations are also expected to be skilled in these methods and to employ them. Sometimes they are reserved for "special meetings." In many congregations an invitation publicly to "accept Christ" and to present oneself for church membership is a regular feature of morning and evening Sunday services.

"Evangelism" and "revivals" have been accompanied by significant even though often unobserved changes in theology.

They presuppose the ability of all to repent and thereby to be "saved"—i.e., to enter upon that eternal life which is the gift of God's grace. For Methodists this has not constituted a serious theological problem: John Wesley's "Arminianism" with its joyous conviction that every human being has enough free will to accept God's offer of salvation in Christ made this kind of evangelism natural and imperative. For those of the Augustinian theology which has prevailed in Reformed and Lutheran bodies, notably those who have found in Calvin an authoritative statement of Christian theology, evangelism poses a difficult problem. This has been true particularly of Congregationalists, Presbyterians, and many Baptists—bodies which in the United States by tradition have believed in Divine election to salvation, irresistible grace, and the perseverance of the saints. If these doctrines are held, of what use is it to urge men to repent and believe? The struggle with this issue was one of the causes of the departure of most Congregationalists from them. The majority of Presbyterians, with the endorsement by their official bodies of the Westminster Confession, theoretically hold to them but for the most part in practice have quietly ignored them. The largest of the Presbyterian bodies, the Presbyterian Church in the U.S.A., while adhering to the Westminster Confession, recognizes the command to make disciples of all nations and the obligation of all believers to aid in "the extension of the Kingdom of Christ throughout the whole earth." Large numbers of Baptists are in churches which proclaim the real freedom of men to accept or reject the Gospel: in time, all but a small minority, most of them "Primitive" (often called colloquially the "Hard Shell") Baptists, have in fact cherished this conviction. This assumption that all men have the full ability to repent and to accept God's gracious offer of salvation through Christ is general among the major and many of the numerically less prominent Protestant denominations in the United States, particularly those longer in the country. Officially several still subscribe to the doctrine of God's election of some for salvation and, by implication or expressly, His determination that others will not be so chosen. In practice, however, the effort is made to win all to the faith and to aim at nothing short of bringing the entire population to a sincere and intelligent commitment to the Gospel. This is shared by the Roman Catholic Church, for it desires to bring every human being, whether non-Christian or professedly Christian, into its fold.

The attainment of the objective of completing the mission of conversion, both of the de-Christianized and of those of non-Christian ancestry, is furthered by another characteristic of the Christianity of the United States, the social stratification of the churches. In the variety presented by Christianity, unequalled in any other country, quite without any planning from a central authority, each denomination tends to appeal to a particular social, racial, or ethnic group. As we have seen, immigrants found in the church with which they were affiliated in Europe one of the few institutions which was familiar and which provided a congenial means of association with those of their kind. Members of the second or third generation, now using English and partly assimilated to the new environment, may join other churches—through marriage, geographic convenience, or conviction—or may drift from any church connexion. However, they tend to stay by the church of their forefathers. In general Negroes, chiefly by their own choice but reinforced by the race feeling of the whites, are affiliated either with exclusively Negro denominations or with congregations in prevailingly white denominations made up only of Negroes. To a large extent the Indian minority are in Indian congregations, although most of the latter are of denominations which are predominantly white. As we have also seen, some denominations are composed chiefly, even though not by deliberate purpose, of the highly educated and those of upper incomes, others of middle-income groups, and still others of much lower-income groups and with few university graduates. For those of the lowest levels of income and education who have a Protestant background there are denominations, some of them called "store front" churches, informal and emotional. Thus all ethnic, racial, and social groups are covered. The gulf which exists in much of Europe between the Church and the labourers in industries and mines with its concomitant hostility of labour to the Church either is absent or is not so deep.

A contributing factor is the middle-class mentality of the people of the United States. There is no aristocracy in the European sense of that term. While there are social strata, most of those in the upper levels have risen by their own efforts from the lower levels or are from ancestors who have so risen, and it is assumed that any one with ambition and determination can do likewise. Class distinctions as they are known in Europe either do not exist in the United States or are less pronounced. The stratification of society is by other categories and with the exception of the cleavage between Negroes and whites is less striking.

Another distinctive feature of the religious life of the United States is the denominations which are not imported but which have had their origin in that country. For the most part, but by no means entirely, those which are most distinctive are from the older, predominantly Anglo-Saxon stock. Some arose from dissatisfaction with the many divisions among Christians which are so much a feature of the United States. Several, springing up quite independently of one another, eschewing denominational designations, have called themselves simply Christians or Disciples of Christ and have sought to go back of what they deem man-made corruptions of the Gospel to the Bible and to base their beliefs and practices on what they find there. Others, holding that God still guides through inspired prophets, maintain that through them come fresh revelations from Him. That has been the conviction of the Mormons. Their name, the Church of Jesus Christ of Latter-Day Saints, reflects the belief that, the various churches having become apostate, God was restoring the true Church through Joseph Smith and that there have been prophets in succession to him. While Christian Scientists would probably not call Mary Baker Eddy a prophet, they hold that through her fresh and authentic light has been shed on the meaning of the teachings of Christ. The expectation of the early return of Christ and the inauguration of his millennial reign has been the inspiration of the Seventh-Day Adventists and Jehovah's Witnesses. Numbers of other denominations, most of them much smaller than these and several of them of recent origin, are in part protests against what they hold to be the degeneracy of the older churches and are attempts to return to the purity of the Gospel. Several of them stress the continued operation of the Holy Spirit showing itself in a second blessing beyond conversion, or in a renewal of the gift of tongues, or in healing, or in a combination of two or more of these. Religious liberty and the sense of being in a new country with its opportunities for beginning afresh and in a better way than in the "old world" have contributed to the emergence of these groups.

The newness of the country and the challenge of its great undeveloped resources help to account for another characteristic of the Christianity of the United States which has often been remarked, its "activism." The churches, whether Protestant, Roman Catholic, or Eastern, have given themselves more to action than to reflection. They have been so intent upon keeping pace, and more than keeping pace, with the nation's growth, with holding the professing Christians and winning the de-Christianized and the non-Christians, and with building churches, both physical plants and ecclesiastical organizations, that they have developed few great theologians. There has been much more theological thought, some of it creative and of high quality and most of it in Protestantism, than is usually recognized. Yet action, skill in developing and utilizing new methods of approach, and attempts to influence the life of local communities and the nation have loomed larger than eminence in theology. This fact is seen, among other ways, in a greater growth in voluntary forms of religious education of youth, including the Sunday School, and in other organized ways of enlisting and holding youth, especially in Protestantism, than in any other country. It is in the United States, for example, that the Young People's Societies for Christian Endeavour had their origin and most extensive spread, and that the Young Men's and Young Women's Christian Associations have attained their largest dimensions.

Associated with the emphasis upon action has been the very large share of laymen and women in the churches and in other frankly Christian movements and organizations. This is true whether in the local parish, in the community, in the state, or in the nation as a whole. The laity have played and still play a very prominent role. Even in the Roman Catholic Church, where the hierarchy successfully asserted its control after an initial struggle with lay "trusteeism," there are many organizations maintained by lay support. In Protestantism lay participation and leadership have been particularly marked. Not only was the most widely influential American "evangelist," Dwight L. Moody, a layman and without formal theological education, and not merely is he who has been the outstanding American in world-wide Christianity, John R. Mott, a layman who has never been enrolled in a theological school, but also there have been thousands of men and women who, unlike these two, have not given their full time to what is often called "religious work" but have devoted much energy to the Church and to its related institutions and organizations.

Likewise akin to the place given to action have been the efforts to improve society as a whole, not only in the United States but also in the world at large. They have arisen from at least two sources. One has been what we have again and again mentioned, the challenge to build afresh and ideally in the "new world." The other has been the tradition of some of the Christian groups which, although minorities, did much to shape the ideals of the country in the early days of colonial settlement and which dreamed of building in this fresh beginning fully Christian societies. Especially important were the Puritans and Independents in New England and the Quakers in Pennsylvania and elsewhere. That strain has continued and has had many expressions. It has taken form in movement after movement, including notably that which emancipated the slaves and that which has sought for the freedmen equal opportunity with the whites for education, livelihood, and social status. On the international scene it has contributed to the formation and maintenance of the League of Nations and its successor, the United Nations. While, latterly, especially after the two world wars of the twentieth century, something of the pessimism of Western Europe has proven contagious and has reinforced the sobering effect of the mounting responsibilities of the United States in a highly perilous and revolutionary world, there remains in many church circles the dream of a better world and the determination to help make that dream a reality.

We have thus far spoken chiefly of the churches of Anglo-Saxon background and have said comparatively little of those from the continent of Europe. If we are to preserve the proportion as it is in the historical and contemporary scene, that is as it should be. The majority of all church members and the overwhelming majority of Protestants are in the former group. Moreover, having been in the country earlier, these churches have more extensively responded to the environment and have tended to set the pattern for the religious life of the nation. Yet we must also say something, even though not as much, of the churches in the latter category.

Of the Protestant churches from the continent of Europe we have already made some mention. Organizationally they are chiefly grouped according to the nation of their origin and, of course, by confessions. By far the most numerous are the Lutherans. They claim something over five million members. In general the Lutheranism of the United States lacks the extreme liberal strain that is here and there prominent in Europe. Its theological conservatism may be due in part to its seeking to hold its constituency in an overwhelmingly non-Lutheran environment in which, in contrast to its predominance and favoured position in Scandinavia and Northern Germany, it is a minority, for the most part of the fairly recent immigration. The theological conservatism may also be attributable to the fact that the liberals in the mother lands did not have sufficient missionary conviction to undertake the arduous task of gathering into churches and holding to the faith the immigrants of Lutheran background in the difficult and unfamiliar environment in the United States. This was done, rather, by men of conservative theology, some of them with a conservatism reinforced by Pietist conviction and enthusiasm.

We must pause to comment, even though briefly, on the Roman Catholic Church in the United States. At mid-century it has a little over a third of those reported to have a formal connexion with one or another of the Christian churches. Unlike its status in the lands from which most of its constituency has stemmed, where it is in the large majority, it is a minority, even though a large one. Arising chiefly from the nineteenth-century immigration, most of it poverty-stricken on its arrival and looked upon by many of the older white stock as un-American, it was long on the defensive, with a persecution complex. It has not completely lost that mentality. However, since, beginning in 1914, the immigrant stream has been greatly reduced and the generations of American birth have begun to share in the prosperity of the country, the Roman Catholic Church has grown in wealth. Perhaps partly because it is still self-conscious and partly because of its traditional imperial temper, it has become more aggressive and its hierarchy dreams of winning the country. Yet, in contrast with much of Europe, where its strength is more in rural sections than in cities, in the United States its immigrant constituency, finding employment in industry and mines, is chiefly urban and is subject to the secularizing pressures of "modern mass society" and to a falling birth rate. Percentage-wise its recent growth has been slightly less than that of Protestantism and it is barely holding its own. Dominant in it are those of Irish or German ancestry. These were the two nationalities which first swelled the Roman Catholic ranks. Moreover, because of their situation on the other side of the Atlantic where they have been faced with a strong Protestantism, they have been more zealous in their faith than have those from Southern Europe.

The Roman Catholicism of the United States, like Protestantism, is activistic. Thus far it has produced much less theological scholarship than has the latter. Like the latter, although more tardily, and not as yet in as large numbers, it is sending missionaries to other parts of the world. It has a body of clergy, sisters, and lay brothers who as a rule are hard-working and devoted. Through its schools, from the elementary level through universities, it is taxing itself to support an educational system in which its faith will be an integral part that thus an informed and loyal laity shall be assured and its professional staff be recruited and trained. Yet no native-born Catholic has been canonized, and the type of sanctity thus commended by Rome does not seem to be emerging in any striking fashion.

How far, if at all, is the Christianity of the United States drawing together? In what ways, if any, is that vision of the unity of all believers in Christ which has been cherished from the very beginning of the faith and which is found in the recorded words of Jesus being realized? In the United States, as we have seen, Christianity displays the greatest variety in organization, doctrine, practice, and tradition that it has ever shown in any one country. Is the professed allegiance to Christ which is common to them all drawing together those who bear his name? Here progress can be reported, but it is far from consummated and it has little prospect of being fully attained. It is taking place in a number of ways.

To enter into an adequate description of the many movements in the United States towards the unity of Christians would require a large volume. We must content ourselves with the bare mention of the chief categories into which they fall.

There is the fusion into a single ecclesiastical structure of two or more denominations. It is mounting, but thus far it has been confined to the union of very similar bodies, such as the Methodist Church from three Methodist churches, the Evangelical United Brethren from two churches of Methodist polity and temper in a constituency which is prevailingly of German background, the Evangelical and Reformed Church from two predominantly German bodies in which the Reformed tradition is strong, and the Congregational Christian Churches of bodies with a Congregational polity. Conversations between churches of quite different polities, prominent among them those between Presbyterians and Episcopalians, have not yet issued in completed action. Nothing as inclusive as the United Church of Canada has yet been achieved.

Another form of unity is by coöperation through councils of churches. These councils are on city, state, and national levels. They are increasing rapidly and are several times more numerous than in any other country. The National Council of the Churches of Christ in the United States of America, formally constituted in 1950, in size of staff and ecclesiastical comprehensiveness is by far the most impressive of those national coöperative bodies which are one of the striking features of Christianity in the twentieth century. More of the financial support of the International Missionary Council and the World Council of Churches comes from the United States than from all other sources. In many cities ministerial associations bring clergy together for fellowship and action.

Non-ecclesiastical organizations bearing the Christian name draw into their membership men and women and boys and girls from many churches. Outstanding are the Young Men's and Young Women's Christian Associations. On their rolls are found not only Protestants of almost all denominations but also Roman Catholics and Orthodox.

The National Conference of Christians and Jews, begun by Protestants, enlists Protestants, Roman Catholics, and Jews in an effort, not at union, but at more sympathetic understanding of one another and the removal of irrational and emotional prejudice.

In rapidly growing communities, usually suburban, Protestant churches in which those of widely differing denominational connexions and backgrounds have membership are multiplying. Some are frankly community churches, without denominational affiliation. Others have a denominational connexion and name. A few, usually in rural areas or towns of declining populations, are local federations of existing congregations of different denominations.

There is an extensive shifting of membership from one denomination to another, probably more than in any other country. Much of this is through marriage, for, in the fluid state of society and in the tax-supported schools young people of widely different ecclesiastical ancestry are brought together. Much is by geographic propinquity: on shifting their residence thousands find it more convenient to worship and work in a congregation other than one of the denomination in which they were reared. Some is from preference for another form of worship. A good deal is from considerations of social prestige. Some is from profound religious conviction.

As we have suggested, unity, although growing, is far from complete. In general the Roman Catholic Church holds aloof. It would like to draw all Christians into its fold. Each year it has thousands of converts, mostly from Protestantism, the majority through marriage. While comprehensive accurate statistics are not available, almost certainly it annually loses many more to Protestantism than it gains. These losses are also largely through marriage, but they are by no means entirely so. Yet there is not the slightest indication that the Roman Catholic constituency is to be fully absorbed into Protestantism. Much the same may be said of the Eastern Churches, although some of them are in predominantly Protestant coöperative organizations. Moreover, bodies having a substantial proportion of the Protestants of the country are not in the comprehensive coöperative movements. Thus the largest of the Baptist groups, the Southern Baptist Convention, is not in them, nor are some of the Lutheran synods. Many Fundamentalists believe that the National Council of Churches and the World Council of Churches have compromised the faith and therefore they refuse to join. Some even denounce these organizations and those in them as "apostate." Although the majority of Protestants are in churches which are members of the World Council of Churches, a much larger minority, as we have said, remain outside than in Europe.

Yet both in coöperating and in non-coöperating churches there is much interpenetration of one by the other, some of it scarcely conscious. As is to be expected because of its greater flexibility, that is more marked in Protestantism than in the Roman Catholic Church and the Eastern Churches. Much use is made of the hymns of other denominations. In the most widely circulated semi-official hymnal of one large Protestant body which refuses to coöperate with other denominations there are more hymns by others than its members than by its members, and the authors range all the way from Roman Catholics to Unitarians. Liturgical forms are spreading, largely of Catholic, although not necessarily Roman Catholic, provenance. The Book of Common Prayer is treasured by many Protestants outside the Protestant Episcopal Church. Among the more devout, books of devotion are prized which arise from many different denominations, Protestant, Roman, and Eastern. Among Protestants such methods as the Sunday School are almost universal. Nearly all Protestant missionary organizations have much the same patterns and there are similarities to them in the Roman Catholic missionary movement. Jews, Roman Catholics, and Protestants, usually at the invitation of a Protestant council of churches, join in community services on the national Thanksgiving Day. Moreover, in some issues, national and international, usually on Protestant initiative, Jews, Roman Catholics, and Protestants act jointly and speak concurrently.

In summary it may be said that in the United States Christianity is taking a distinct form. Predominantly Protestant of non-Anglican Anglo-Saxon provenance, it yet presents a variety in which all the current historic forms of Christianity are represented. These are by no means fully drawn together into one structure, whether of organization, doctrine, or worship. Yet they have come to present a fairly common family likeness arising in part from the activism made necessary by winning a place for themselves in a new environment in which de-Christianization is threatened and little or no support comes from a state which, while friendly, is religiously neutral. An increasing proportion of the population is being drawn into at least a formal connexion with one or another of the churches. In spite of tensions, coöperation is growing and consciously or unconsciously and in varying degrees every church is learning from the others.

Partly because of the mounting percentage of the population which is enrolled in the churches, there is danger that the Christianity of the country will be an expression of "the American way of life" and will become ancillary to it. At least some European observers have declared it to be absorbed into the community and but little differentiated from it. As millions are drawn into the churches, discipline is relaxed and the local congregations tend to become social organizations with a religious tinge, only slightly unlike the many "service clubs" and fraternal orders which flourish in the American scene. Yet minorities in the churches, among them some of the outstanding officials, protest against this conformation to the national pattern. From time to time spokesmen for the churches, such as the national denominational assemblies and the National Council of Churches in the United States of America, raise their voices in protest against trends and policies in the country and the government and seek positively to call the country to constructive goals and action. They are aware that if Christians are to be worthy of the name they are "not to be conformed to this world," but are to be "transformed."

Although a Christianity is emerging in the United States which is distinctive of that land, the vast majority of those who are associated with the churches hold to the core of the faith, even though in the case of most of them with only slight comprehension of its meaning. That core is centred around Jesus Christ as the incarnation of the eternal God, fully God and fully man, in whom God, who is self-giving love, has sought and through His Holy Spirit continues to seek men to save them from their sin, and to work in them a new birth into eternal life in likeness to Christ in fellowship with Himself and with one another in the community of the redeemed which is His Church—the Church which in this present age is imperfect and outwardly divided, but which in that age which is to come beyond history and time is to be consummated in perfect likeness to its Lord. The bodies which do not hold to this conviction enroll only a small minority of the Christians of the United States. Those which modify it sharply are somewhat larger but still are a small proportion of the whole. The fact of this adherence is especially important because of the increasing share which the churches of the United States have in spreading the Christian faith outside the Occident.

CHAPTER IV

The Response of Christianity in Non-Occidental Peoples and Their Cultures

WHAT is the response of Christianity to the peoples and cultures outside the Occident? What response are these peoples and cultures giving to Christianity? Until recently Christianity has been confined almost entirely to the Occident. To be sure, it began in Asia, but it quickly moved into the Hellenistic and Latin worlds. In its first few centuries it won followings among several peoples clear across Asia and in Africa. A few peoples in these regions adopted it as their community or national religion—among them the Armenians, the Copts, and the Ethiopians. Yet the Moslem tide checked it, eliminated many Christian communities, and reduced others to encysted minorities, on the defensive and slowly losing ground. In South India, outside the Islamic world, a few tens of thousands persisted, but, responding to the Hindu environment, were like a distinct caste, neither reaching out for converts nor losing many. Five centuries ago very few Christians were to be found outside Europe. They were seen in a few places in Western Asia, in Africa north of the Sahara, and in South India. But Christianity was almost entirely a European religion.

Then began a phenomenal spread which has continued into our day. It has been in connexion with the expansion of European peoples, mostly Western Europeans. It has taken place partly through migrations of European peoples, predominantly to the Americas, Australasia, and South Africa, and partly through missions among non-Europeans. Until the closing decade of the eighteenth century these missions were chiefly Roman Catholic. Then, in the nineteenth century, came a fresh burst of expansion and most of the world was brought under the domination of European peoples, both those traditionally Protestant and Roman Catholic, but mainly the former. That domination was political, economic, and cultural. Latterly non-European peoples have been throwing off the political yoke and are striving for economic emancipation. But they are doing this largely by devices derived from the Occident. The spread of Occidental culture and of ideologies first formulated in the Occident continues, and at an accelerated pace. Industrialization by processes devised in the West is mounting. Forms of education first developed in the West are being adopted. Occidental political institutions, with modifications, are being copied, and democracy as Western Europeans know it and Communism, first formulated in Western Europe, are moving across the earth. A vast revolution is under way which is either profoundly altering or sweeping aside non-Occidental cultures. It is in association with these developments that Christianity has become world-wide. In the past century and a half it has been spread by both Roman Catholics and Protestants—in comparison with what had been done before 1800 more by the latter than the former. Today there are Christians, most of them gathered in churches, in almost every tribe and nation. Nearly everywhere they are minorities, but with few exceptions these have been and are growing.

What forms are these Christian minorities taking? To what degree is the Christianity which they embody the same and to what degree does it differ from that in the Occident? In what fashion and to what extent are non-Occidental cultures outside churches responding to Christianity? These are the questions to which we must address ourselves in the next few pages. Full answers would demand at least a large volume, but, as in our earlier chapters, in the short space to which we must confine ourselves we may be able to suggest the most important.

In the shaping of the Christianity of these minorities and in the response of the cultures to Christianity several factors enter. One is the kind of Christianity which has been introduced. It is either Roman Catholic or Protestant or both. Except in Japan, North China, India, Alaska, and the Near East, Eastern Churches have had no share and there only a minor one. Roman Catholicism is less flexible than Protestantism, is directed from a common authoritative centre, Rome, but varies somewhat with the country from which it comes and the order or congregation by which it is brought in and nourished. Protestantism responds more easily to its environment and differs markedly according to the country of its provenance and the agency by which it is spread. Another factor is the culture, including the religion, of the peoples among whom these churches, mostly young, are found. Here there is very great variety. In general the cultures are divided into "primitive," with religions which are "animistic," and "advanced," in which the religions are "high." These last are much further from unanimity than are the animistic ones, and the latter are by no means all the same. A third factor is the impact of non-religious aspects of the Occident. This also is diverse, because of its many-sidedness and because of the country or countries which predominate in its introduction. A fourth factor is the response made to the total impact of the Occident. In some cultures, most of them "primitive," there is rapid disintegration. In others resistance is more marked and change is slower. In all there is what we may call nationalism, in the broadest sense of that term, namely, a collective self-consciousness and pride with resentment against foreign aggression, heightened by contact with the nationalism of the West. A fifth factor is the degree to which the Christian minorities are knit into the world-wide Christian fellowship, either through the Roman Catholic Church or through the prevailingly but not exclusively Protestant Ecumenical Movement. Such integration will clearly make for the preservation of the Christian faith as the West has known it. The lack of it, including rebellion against it, will work towards departure from Christianity as it has been transmitted through the Occident.

We must expand a little what we have suggested about the channels through which Christianity is transmitted. Particularly in the present century, both the Roman Catholic Church and the Protestant agencies have stressed the development of indigenous leadership. There has been a continuing conviction that only thus can the faith be firmly rooted among any people, and latterly a realization that the rising tides of nationalism, directed as they are against any hint of Western imperialism in any form, will be hostile to organizations, religious or secular, dominated by foreigners. Since World War I Roman Catholics have registered great progress in raising up an indigenous priesthood and in elevating some of its members to the episcopate. Protestants have made similar advances. The rate of transfer to indigenous control has varied from country to country and from missionary agency to missionary agency. Thus in Africa south of the Sahara Roman Catholics have been slower in attaining that goal than in

India, Indochina, China, the Philippines, and Japan. In Indonesia Protestant missionaries, predominantly Dutch and German, had effected but little transfer of authority until World War II forced their hands. Because of a combination of national sensitivity, the ability of the Japanese Christians, and the exigencies of World War II, in the Land of the Rising Sun both Roman Catholics and Protestants made a complete transfer to indigenous clergy earlier than in any other country. In Protestant circles after the defeat of Japan the coming of many new organizations, almost all of them without much previous missionary experience, has set back advance towards that goal. In most of such congregations as they have gathered, foreigners, mainly Americans, still exercise authority.

Both Roman Catholics and Protestants have encouraged indigenous expressions of the faith in art, architecture, music, hymns, and festivals. In some of this activity foreigners have taken the initiative and have gone more rapidly than the local Christians. For example, in some instances they have wished to erect churches in the traditional architecture of the land when their native colleagues have objected on the ground that this is associated with the paganism from which the Christians have emerged. However, in much of the utilization of inherited forms, whether in painting, sculpture, music, or poetry, Christians of the country have been the creators.

In preventing wide formal departures from the faith as they hold it Roman Catholics have been more successful than have Protestants, partly because of the hierarchical structure, controlled as their church is by the clergy under an episcopate authoritatively directed from the Vatican. This success is also partly, but probably somewhat less, due to the emphasis in many missions upon a prolonged catechumenate with careful instruction. In contrast, a basic Protestant principle is the priesthood of all believers with the concomitant one of the right and the duty of each Christian to interpret the Scriptures —although with respect for the convictions of other believers of both the past and the present. While ecclesiastical authority often frowns upon applying these principles in an extreme manner, the attitude which they engender makes for independent, often immature, thought and action. The lack of a single centre which can speak and act decisively for all Protestantism also permits wide diversity.

As a result, schisms in the Roman Catholic Church outside the Occident have been few and conspicuous heresies almost entirely absent. To be sure, pre-Christian superstitions and practices have often survived, and Christian moral standards have frequently been lowered, but as a rule with outward compliance with the dogmas of the Church and respect for the authority of the hierarchy. The latter may have winked at these compromises and even at times have sought to guide them, but the unity of the Church in doctrine, sacrament, and structure has generally been preserved. In recent times the chief exception has been the secession of several hundred thousand Filipinos in the 1890's through the Independent Catholic Church of the Philippines, led by Aglipay. This was in protest against the refusal of Rome to bow to the demand of Filipino nationalism for the immediate creation of a hierarchy of Filipinos. With it went a liberal, Unitarian theology. In China in the 1950's the Communists have attempted to bring into being a national Catholic church which will hold to most of the Catholic doctrines and rites but will disavow loyalty to Rome—which the Communists denounce as "imperialistic."

In contrast, many movements have emerged from Protestantism. Some of these have departed widely from the central affirmations of the Christian faith. Among them have been the Hau Hau or Pai Marire cult among the Maoris of New

Zealand and the T'ai P'ing Rebellion in China in the nineteenth century, and in the twentieth century most of the multitudinous Bantu sects in South Africa, some of the prophet movements in Africa south of the Sahara, and in the same region the Watch Tower Movement inspired by Jehovah's Witnesses. Others are more nearly in accord with historic Christianity. Such have been the Jesus Family in China and the groups, usually of highly educated men and women, which have arisen in Japan in consequence of the lectures, writings, and teaching of the Bible by Kanso Uchimura; members of the latter usually are unbaptized and have no connexion with any ecclesiastical body.

It may be pertinent to ask whether the emergence of a larger variety of movements from Protestantism than from Roman Catholicism, some of them far from the central core of the Christian faith, is evidence of greater vitality. Is the Roman Catholic form of the faith among non-Occidental peoples more passive than Protestantism and therefore less vigorous? That would be difficult either to prove or to disprove. For the thesis we note the situation in Latin America where the numerical fruits of Roman Catholic missions among the Indians are larger than in any other population of non-European ancestry. Here, as we have noted, is a body of Roman Catholics, white, Indian, Negro, and mixed, which constitutes a little more than a third of those the world over who are counted as Roman Catholics. They are orthodox in doctrine and submissive to Papal direction. Yet they have produced no major theologian or religious order and are so far from supplying their own priests that they have only about 7 per cent of the total clergy of the Roman Catholic Church and depend upon Europe and the United States to make up the deficit. In contrast, in at least one Latin-American country, Brazil, many Protestant converts and their descendants are enthusiastic in propagating their faith. We recall, too, that in India and China at the end of the eighteenth century, when the supply of missionaries from Europe dwindled, the number of Roman Catholics shrank or remained stationary and their morale declined. On the other hand, we remember the perseverance of Roman Catholic Christianity in Japan when for two and a half centuries persecution drove it underground and cut it off from contacts with its fellow believers in other countries. As witness to vigour in Protestantism, we do well to remark the rapidly growing place which members of its "younger churches" in Asia and Africa are taking in various phases of the Ecumenical Movement in meetings, administration, and thought. It may be significant, too, that this is in spite of the fact that Protestant missions outside the Occident and the churches arising from them are, on the whole, much more recent than Roman Catholic missions and, accordingly, have had less time to become deeply rooted and to stimulate creative life.

As we have suggested, the cultures outside the Occident in which Christianity has spread fall roughly into two groups, "primitive" and "advanced." We must say something about the response to Christianity of each.

For the most part, as was to be expected, the spread of Christianity has been most rapid among peoples of "primitive" cultures. For many centuries they have been less resistant to the impact of "advanced" cultures than has been one "advanced" culture to another "advanced" culture. Their religions have yielded to a "high" religion much more readily than has one "high" religion to another. Here we note the ease with which Islam quickly won the allegiance of the majority of the Arabs and recall that at the time of Mohammed most Arabs had a religion not far removed from "primitivism." We bear in mind, too, the fact that the conversion to Buddhism of the

Ceylonese, Burmese, Tibetans, and Mongols occurred when the religions of these peoples were not far removed from animism. In contrast, in India, where it faced Brahminism (Hinduism), which mixed animism and crude polytheism with profound philosophy, Buddhism was eventually absorbed and all but disappeared, and in China, where the ground was preempted by the indigenous Confucianism and Taoism, it never succeeded in eliminating its rivals but simply gained acceptance as one of several faiths. In somewhat similar fashion, Christianity has latterly gathered converts most extensively among folk of "primitive" cultures, aided by the disintegration of these cultures induced by other forms of impact from the Occident.

The rapid spread of Christianity among "primitive" peoples is seen in many parts of the world. Except in the remote fastnesses of the mountains and valleys of South America, the large majority of the Indians of the New World profess the Christian faith. In the United States the proportion is mounting. In the Pacific most of the Polynesians and Micronesians have been Christians for about a century, and the faith is spreading among the islands which go to make up Melanesia. Most of the Filipinos, then animists or near-animists, accepted the Christian faith from Spanish Roman Catholic missionaries in the sixteenth and seventeenth centuries and in the sense in which that designation is usually employed constitute the one Christian nation in the Far East. In Indonesia the faith has been and is spreading very rapidly among the animistic elements of the population. Latterly the most striking gains have been among the animistic Bataks of Sumatra. Yet only slight advance has been achieved among the Moslem majority of Indonesia and the Hindus of Bali. The past hundred years and especially the years since World War I have seen a mounting tide of conversions in the prevailingly animistic Africa south of the Sahara, brought about in most of the areas under British control more through Protestants than Roman Catholics. In regions under Roman Catholic governments the accessions to that form of the faith have been greater than those to Protestantism. On the continent of Asia the numerical advances of Christianity in the nineteenth and twentieth centuries have been most marked among folk of a "primitive" or near-"primitive" cultural level. Thus in India, outside the enclaves under Portuguese rule and those stemming from them and apart from the ancient communities of Syrian Christians and the sections of those communities which have submitted to Rome, the majority of the Christians are from the animistic tribes of the hills and jungles and the depressed, near-animistic "outcastes." This is true of both Roman Catholics and Protestants. The gains have been very rapid in the present century, notably by Protestants. In Burma only a few thousand converts have been from among the numerically and politically dominant Buddhists. In contrast, tens of thousands have come from the Karens, a people who, when the first Protestant missionaries reached them, were without a written language and were animists. Significantly large accessions have also been from among other animistic but less numerous peoples of Burma.

As if to invalidate this generalization, in Indochina until the war between the French and the Communist Vietminh Roman Catholics were multiplying and on the eve of World War II numbered not far from a million and a half. Most of these converts have been from among peoples whose culture has been tinctured with Confucianism or Buddhism and who could scarcely be called "primitives." Yet the elements of the population from which most of the accessions have come have more of animism than of Confucianism or Buddhism in their religious conceptions and practices.

From the standpoint of the modifications made in the faith

among the Christians drawn from "primitive," animistic backgrounds, it is significant that conversions have been largely by
"mass movements" of a natural social group, whether that be
a tribe, a village, or what among the depressed of India corre-
sponds to a caste. This situation has similarities to what took
place on a larger scale in the Roman Empire after Constantine
and his successors espoused Christianity. It is also akin to the
conversion, some years earlier, of the Armenians and to the
processes of conversion of the peoples of Europe after the decline of the Roman Empire.

Obviously in the group conversions of those of animistic
background, except for a few, comprehension of the nature
and meaning of the Gospel will come slowly. Even though
careful and prolonged catechetical instruction is given before
and after baptism, as by many Roman Catholic missionaries in
Africa, though, as among Protestants, translation of the Bible
into the vernacular is accompanied by teaching the Christians
and their children to read, and though, as in many places,
hymns become popular and the Gospel sings its way into the
hearts of the Christians, inner apprehension and full, intelligent commitment may be greatly delayed. Many will believe
that being a Christian means abandoning certain religious
rites and practices, conforming to the ones associated with the
new faith, and obeying a few ethical precepts. They will expect
of Christianity what they had learned to demand of the pre-
Christian rites, such as protection from disease or other mis-
fortune for themselves, their families, and their domestic
animals.

Europeans and those of European descent should be the last
to criticize the persistence of pre-Christian attitudes, for most
of their ancestors came into the faith in much the same way.
Indeed, the fruits of that mass conversion, both good and bad,
are still being reaped. The formal adherence of practically all

the population of Western Europe to the faith brought a permeation of society with ethical standards derived from Christian sources, a conception of the worth of the individual, and
extensive care for the unfortunate. Presumably the Occident
has been better for the common subscription to Christianity
instead of having it represented only by minorities, even
though those minorities might be intelligently dedicated to the
Gospel. Indeed, the two approaches have not been mutually
exclusive. There has been and in some countries still is the
almost universal compliance with the Christian rites of baptism, confirmation, marriage, and burial, together with groups,
sometimes monastic but more often non-monastic, fully committed to Christ. Yet the superficiality and conventionality of
the adherence of the majority have made for hypocrisy and a
callous disregard of Christian standards.

We must also note again the wide aberrations which have
developed in some of the peoples of recent "primitive" ancestry who have borne the Christian name. Outstanding have
been the Bantu sects of South Africa which we have already
mentioned. In South Africa a substantial proportion of the
blacks, mostly Bantus, are professedly Christians and Protestants. Among these Bantus, Protestant Christian sects have
proliferated. In 1953 they numbered about thirteen hundred
as against about eight hundred in 1946 and were reported to
have over a million members. Several causes have contributed
to their multiplication. One is desire for freedom from control
by white missionaries. In a land where the Africans have so
few institutions which they can call their own, here is a way of
asserting independence. Another is the rebellion of some African clergymen against discipline, perhaps for a moral offense,
meted out by a missionary or a church body. Still another is
the desire of an individual for power, a desire which finds
expression in gathering around him in the name of religion a

group which he can control. It is also suggested that a factor may be the tribal tradition. It was in the tribe that the individual found fellowship and security. In the cities of South Africa the tribe has no place and the individual is uprooted and cast adrift. These sects, most of them comparatively small, constitute a partial substitute for the tribe. Most of the African prophets of which we have spoken, the movements which they have headed, and the Watch Tower Movement owe their inception in part to Christianity, usually in one or another of its Protestant forms, but have departed more or less widely from the core of the faith. Many African Christians question and even abandon monogamy.

A somewhat different set of problems is found among the Christians from the outcastes of India. It is not easy to bring them up from their filth and low sex morals to an approximation to Christian standards. That, however, can be and often is accomplished through careful instruction and supervision by the missionary. In some respects more baffling is the mentality which has been bred by generations of subservience to the socially superior members of society. Accustomed to poverty, to the lowest menial tasks, to contumely, to dependence, and to being discouraged from any initiative, they transfer that dependence to the mission and the missionary. Leadership among them is slow to develop. When it emerges it may be rash, restive under advice, demanding, and the source of difficulty and embarrassment to the missionary.

Among the Karens in Burma another complication has arisen. Their Christianity has been a symbol and bond of racial particularism and has contributed to heightening the friction between themselves and the dominant Burmese. That friction, as is well known, broke out into open insurrection after the expulsion of the Japanese at the close of World War II. Christianity has been the inspiration and the means of giving education to thousands of Karens. Their churches are largely self-supporting and self-governing and thus have promoted independence and have given experience in it. Even before World War II the Burmese were looking with disfavour upon the progress of a people whom they had traditionally regarded as inferior. After the Japanese were expelled and Burma broke with Britain, many of the Karens demanded autonomy as a distinct political unit. This led to war.

More striking and more tragic was a movement to which we have referred, that bearing the name of T'ai P'ing. It arose from contacts, slight but decisive, with Protestant literature and personnel, and later made more extended use of what came from Protestants, notably a translation of the Bible. Its leaders would probably not have called it Christian, certainly not in the sense in which that term is understood by Protestants and Roman Catholics. It was a religious-political movement, intent on ruling China. Parallels are to be found in earlier attempts in Chinese history by groups holding to a particular set of religious convictions to seize the realm. There was a notable one by Taoists early in the Christian Era. What distinguished the T'ai P'ings from the others were the ingredients from Christian sources.

Still more tragic has been the capture of China by Communism. Although denouncing all historic religions and insisting that their adherents, while theoretically accorded freedom of belief, subordinate their organizations to the Communist state and coöperate with it on its terms, Communists have a faith, dogmatically held. As is so well known as to be almost a banality, that faith arose in Western Europe and has in it determinative elements derived from Christianity. With some degree of accuracy, it has been called, as was Islam, a Christian heresy. Here, too, the sources, so far as they were Christian, were chiefly Protestant.

The T'ai P'ings and the Communists bring us to the place of Christianity in peoples of "advanced" non-Occidental cultures, for both have been in China, a land of indubitably high civilization, and their leaders were and have been drawn chiefly from the educated. Among these peoples of "advanced" cultures the numerical accessions to the faith constitute small minorities. Conversions have been increasing in the nineteenth and twentieth centuries, but, except in Ceylon and for remnants of pre-Moslem churches in Western Asia and Africa, among none of them do the Christian communities constitute more than 5 per cent of the population. In most of the larger cultural units they are considerably less. However, in each the influence of Christianity is far greater than the size of the Christian churches would indicate and in most of them it is growing. Here is part of the response of the non-Occidental world to Christianity. Although in most countries of high civilization outside the Occident the totals of baptized have been growing, the churches are minorities. Yet in several of these lands there is taking place a permeation by ideals derived from Christianity but fitted into existing or emerging cultural patterns. We can best describe what is happening by considering in succession the several major cultural areas and cultures outside the Occident. Except for the portion of the Moslem world in Africa north and east of the Sahara, all of them are in Asia. We will begin with the Moslem world and move eastward.

In a large part of the Moslem world the numbers of Christians have been declining since the Arab conquest more than a thousand years ago. In the twentieth century that decline has continued. During World War I the Nestorians in Iran were set upon by their foes and thousands either were killed or fled. During that same war the Turks massacred thousands of Armenians, and other thousands of that unhappy people were deported. In 1922 as an aftermath of the conflict between Greece and Turkey tens of thousands of Greek Christians were removed from the latter country to Greece. In Egypt there has been a chronic leakage from the Coptic Church to Islam, although because of the high birth rate of the Copts their total number has not seriously declined. There have been and are extensive Roman Catholic and Protestant missions in the Near East, but the traditional solidarity of Islam and the political and social pressures against apostasy have been effective in preventing many conversions from that faith to Christianity. In Iran a few hundreds have been won. Some have come in Pakistan. A few thousand have been gathered from Moslems in Indonesia. However, in the Near East the Roman Catholics and Protestants are mainly from the Eastern Churches.

Yet through Christian schools and hospitals something of ethical change has been wrought in many individual Moslems. These institutions have been begun and maintained by both Protestants and Roman Catholics. Extensive works of relief have been carried on under the auspices of Christian organizations. Through these institutions and enterprises Christian ideals of character and social service have been taught by word and example. They have inspired hundreds and probably thousands of Moslems to more honest and sacrificial living. Presumably if missions from the Occident were to die out these expressions of the Gospel would eventually disappear. Their vitality depends upon continued currents of life issuing from vigorous churches. The older Eastern Churches are by no means dead. The fact that they have survived after more than a millennium of Moslem rule and the impossibility of recruiting their ranks by conversions is evidence of vitality. Here and there are signs of fresh life. However, their witness does not have much effect on the non-Christians about them.

Yet through contacts with the Christianity of Europe and America there is a kind of response to Christianity which is not negative. It appropriates appreciatively some of the fruits of the Gospel without availing itself of their essential source.

As we move on to India we find a situation which both resembles and differs from that in the Moslem world. Here, too, are well-entrenched "high" religions. Of them Hinduism is dominant, Islam is next, and there are important minorities of Sikhs, Jains, Buddhists, and Parsees. The prevailing climate of opinion is Hindu. Except for minorities, even the inroads of Western secularism have not basically modified it. Those minorities, while influential, have not yet seriously loosened the hold of Hinduism on the country. In a certain sense Hinduism is less intolerant than Islam. It holds that there are many ways to truth and many expressions of the Divine, but that none of them has all the truth and all of them together do not give full knowledge of what in its essence is ultimately unknowable to men. It is willing to make room for all religious faiths which will accommodate themselves to these basic convictions. But it is intolerant of any religion which, like Islam and Christianity, claims to be the final and complete revelation of God. Although there have been rebels against it who have professed to remain loyal to the faith, the social structure centring around caste has seemed to be integral to Hinduism. Indeed, Hinduism is often called Brahminism because of the important place taken in it by the highest caste. Except in Pakistan, where they are the overwhelming majority, Moslems constitute a minority. As is well known, they are the descendants either of invaders or of converts. The converts were mostly from the depressed classes. They saw in the theoretically casteless Islam a way of escape from hereditary obloquy through the adoption of the religion of the conquerors. The Sikhs represent in part the response of India to Islam, for much in their religion appears to have been inspired by contact with that faith. Buddhism and Jainism are survivals of what may be called Hindu "heresies": about twenty-five hundred years ago they sprang from an early stage of Hinduism. The Parsees are a small but wealthy closed group, descendants of Zoroastrian immigrants. From these "high" religions have come only a small proportion of those who in India bear the Christian name. Conversion often means social ostracism and expulsion from the family. Yet these "high" religions have yielded far more converts than has Islam in the Near East.

The Christian churches of India are of several origins. The early history of the Syrian Christians is shrouded in obscurity. The traditional descent from a mission of Thomas, one of the Twelve Apostles, is yet to be proved. More likely seems to be derivation from Nestorian immigrants from Mesopotamia and Persia. By the time when we first have detailed information about them, early in the sixteenth century, the Syrian Christians had so far accommodated themselves to the Indian environment that they had become in effect a closed caste, neither winning accessions from the surrounding paganism nor losing many of their number to it. It was only in the nineteenth century that contact with Protestant, largely Anglican missionaries, led to the separation of a minority, now the Mar Thoma Church, from which have issued active missionary efforts among non-Christians. The Roman Catholics, who constitute the largest body of Christians in India, are in part the descendants of those who accepted the faith through being under Roman Catholic rulers in the territories, such as Goa, which were Portuguese possessions. Theoretically Portuguese, although most of them with very little if any Portuguese blood in their veins, they tend to be proud of their Portuguese name and connexion and to identify them with their Roman Catholic faith. They have spread beyond the borders of the Portu-

guese enclaves and thousands are to be found in other parts
of India. Large bodies of Roman Catholics have been drawn
from the Syrian Christians, some of them as Uniates, keeping
many of their hereditary rites and customs, and some fully
assimilated to Rome and using the Latin rites. Still other
Roman Catholics are converts or the descendants of converts
from non-Christian faiths who have come through the efforts
of missionaries outside the Portuguese domains. A large proportion are from among outcastes and animistic hill folk. The
number of Protestants has been growing more rapidly than
the number of Roman Catholics. They have been drawn from
various caste levels of society. However, the large majority are
from the outcastes and the hill tribes.

In the response of India to Christianity certain features distinctive of that country are to be seen. These we can note
quickly, but their importance is much greater than the brevity
of our summary might indicate.

In contrast with the Moslem world, the total number of
Christians in India has been rapidly mounting. In 1914 about
ten out of a thousand were Christians. In 1950 about twenty-
five out of a thousand were in that category. However, Christians are still only a small minority of the population. More
than half of them are in the South. That means that in most
of the country they are an even smaller minority.

Christians are largely identified with certain social strata
and thus tend to fit into the pattern of caste which is characteristic of Indian society. Some are Syrian Christians, themselves, as we have suggested, in effect a distinct caste. Others
bear the name of Portuguese, and are ingrown, akin to a caste.
Still others are from the outcastes and the hill peoples and,
falling into groups which reflect their origin, are as a whole
in the lowest rung of the social ladder. A sprinkling, in some
places influential, is from the castes, although even here most

are from what might be called a lower stratum of castes, the Sudras. Those from the highest castes are relatively very few. The Church is thus distinctly a class institution. For the most part through its converts of the past century and a half it is made up of the humbler elements. As in the Moslem world, the great majority of the politically, economically, and culturally dominant have held aloof. While not generally as severe as in the Moslem world, the penalties for making the break with their families and caste which is entailed in baptism have been an effective deterrent from that step.

However, as a further response of India to Christianity, much more than in Moslem lands there has been a permeation of society outside the churches with ideas and ideals derived from the Gospel. This has come not only through contact with missions but also through other channels, among them the reading of English literature in connexion with the form of education promoted by the British *raj* and attendance at schools and universities in the British Isles. The contact with missions has been partly through the distribution of literature, particularly the Bible, partly through preaching, partly through acquaintance with individual missionaries, and notably through attendance in Christian schools. In most of these schools the student body has been largely non-Christian, and one of their purposes has been so to infiltrate Indian life that they will be a preparation for the Gospel. Moreover, much more than in the Moslem world the churches themselves have sought to reach non-Christians. One of the outstanding expressions of the zeal for evangelism has been the National Missionary Society of India. Its first secretary was V. Z. Azariah. Later, as the first Indian to be raised to the Anglican episcopate Azariah was zealous and successful in inspiring those under him to win non-Christians.

Fully as varied as the channels through which the Gospel

has moved out into Indian society have been the manifestations of its influence. A few of the more prominent of these may serve as an indication of what a thorough and comprehensive survey would disclose. One of the earliest is the Brahmo Samaj, founded in 1828. While not breaking fully with Hinduism, it has honoured Christ and has been a syncretistic movement in which the chief elements are of Christian and Hindu provenance. Recruited chiefly from the wealthy and educated, it has had a highly influential but numerically small following. In later decades it has waned, but not before there issued from it Rabindranath Tagore, a son of the second leader, who attained world-wide prominence as poet, philosopher, and educator. The Servants of India Society, which has had as its purpose the progress of the nation through the devoted self-giving of its members, appears to have come into being through the example of a mission of one of the Anglican monastic orders. It is said that there are thousands, many of them former students in Christian schools, who think of themselves as Christians but who have never formally broken with their inherited religion by being baptized. How many of them there are cannot be statistically determined. The degree to which their religious and ethical conceptions have been moulded by the Gospel undoubtedly differs with each individual—as, indeed, it does even with all who have made a formal Christian commitment.

Again and again Indians prominent in the political and intellectual life of their nation who are frankly not Christians testify to their debt to Christians and to Christian schools attended in their youth. The most influential Indian of the twentieth century and probably the one whose impact upon his fellow countrymen and the world at large has been wider and deeper than that of any other Indian since Gautama Buddha was M. K. Gandhi. Intellectually he was not the product of Christian schools, but in his youth, while a student in England and during his years in South Africa, he had contacts with Christians, some of them in intimate friendship. He remained a Hindu, was never baptized, and did not think of himself as a Christian. Yet the life, teachings, and death of Jesus made a profound impression on him, and some of his favourite hymns were Christian. To a degree which he himself would probably have found it difficult to appraise, his principles of non-violence and of unselfish devotion to his people were from Jesus. He gave to the ancient Indian term *ahimsa,* "harmlessness," originally negative and passive, a positive and active content which seems to have come from the Gospel. When he perished at the hand of an assassin many Indians declared that he had died a Christlike death. Thus, whether or not they were fully conscious of what they were doing, they acknowledged Christ to be the ideal by whom they were measuring their hero and were gaining some inkling, however slight, of the meaning of the vicarious sufferings and death of Christ. Through Gandhi Christ has been modifying, even if among most of them only to a slight extent, the ethical and religious outlook of millions of Indians. The immediate successor of Gandhi as a political figure, Pandit Jawaharlal Nehru, has regarded religion as an obstacle to the national unity which is his passionate desire. Although a Brahmin, he is frankly a secularist. Yet he has said that his ethical standards stem from Christianity.

Here have been or are movements and men which owe a great debt to Christianity. They are part of the response of India to Christianity. In general those which we have mentioned are within the pattern of Hinduism. They are attempts to adopt elements from Christianity without abandoning the kind of intolerant tolerance which is of the essence of Hinduism. Similar repercussions have been seen among some of the other religions of India. In spite of all the sincerity which has marked them, they either have been blind to the core of the Gospel or, if aware of it, have refused to accept it. Not accepting it, they have missed the source from which have come the features of Christianity which they have adopted and they therefore do not possess that which gives continuing power to what they have admired. If that core is not recognized and adhered to, the outcome will be either that the ideals derived from the Gospel will sooner or later fade out or that they will be so badly distorted as to be baleful.

Indeed, our world is witness to the rapid spread of one of the most tragic of these distortions, Communism. We see it in Europe. We have met it in gigantic dimensions in China. It is present in India. With its specious promises and its skilful propaganda and able organization, it is one of the greatest menaces to the welfare of India and the Indians.

The question inevitably arises as to whether the Church in India is to be sufficiently vibrant with life to win growing numbers to an understanding commitment to the Gospel. Are the older forms, namely, the Syrian and the Roman Catholic so far as it is represented by the "Portuguese" and the Uniates, to be primarily, as in the past, encysted enclaves, conforming to the caste tradition of India and not reaching out much to win converts or to influence the life of the country as a whole? Will the newer Roman Catholic communities and the Protestant churches be any better? At first sight the prospect is not encouraging. Drawn as they have been chiefly from the most underprivileged and the "primitive" or near-"primitive" members of society, they do not seem to constitute promising material. The movements of which we have spoken which issue in part from Christianity but which have departed from its core owe most of such Christian elements as they possess not to these churches but to contacts with missionaries from the Occident and to the literature and institutions through which missionaries have operated. If missionaries were to cease to come would the permeation of the life of India by the Gospel continue, even in the imperfect and distorted ways which we have described? We cannot know. We do know that not only are the newer Christian communities growing but leadership, some of it both able and devoted, is beginning to emerge from them. The prospect is far less bleak and much more encouraging than in the world of Islam.

We must pass rapidly over the prevailingly Buddhist Ceylon. There the proportion of Christians is larger than in India, but the majority of the Christians are Roman Catholics and the strength of that church dates from the days of Portuguese occupation, when, as was true in the Portuguese possessions in India, pressures of various kinds brought about large accessions. In the face of resurgent nationalism, percentage-wise the growth of the churches, while marked, has not kept pace with the striking increase in the population.

Nor need we say much of Burma. There, as we have noted, the cultural patterns have influenced the response to Christianity. Most of the conversions have been from the animistic peoples and tribes. Only a few thousand have been gathered from the dominant majority, the Burmese proper. Loyal to Buddhism, the latter have not gone over in numbers to any other religion. Indeed, the marked revival of Buddhism in the 1940's and 1950's may be in part a reaction against Christianity. The churches tend to be grouped according to the racial patterns of the land.

In Thailand, more solidly Buddhist than Burma and with fewer "primitives," the numerical growth of Christianity has not been marked. In Malaya, with its mixture of Moslem Malays and of Chinese and Indian immigrants, very few converts have come from Islam, and the chief strength of Christianity is among the Chinese. Here again the response to Christianity has been in large part determined by racial and cultural factors.

In China the course of Christianity has been much more intermittent than in India. Christianity was introduced in the seventh century and died out three hundred years or so later. It reëntered in the thirteenth century and had disappeared by the sixteenth century. Brought in once more, by Roman Catholics, late in the sixteenth century, since then it has been continuously present. The Russian Orthodox came in the seventeenth century but have never won large numbers. The first Protestant missionary arrived in 1807, and in the nineteenth and twentieth centuries Protestantism has proportionately grown more rapidly than has either of the other two. However, the Roman Catholic Church, having a head start of more than two centuries, counted about three times as many baptized when the Communist curtain descended. In proportion to the population Christianity is much weaker than in India. In 1950 only about one in a hundred adhered to it. Yet in China, with its fairly homogeneous population and its lack of persistent hereditary class distinctions, Christians have been largely from a cross section of the population and are not so much from the lower rungs of the social ladder as in India. Indeed, under the republic which was inaugurated in 1911–1912 and until the Communists took over the country, Christians, and especially Protestant Christians, have been more prominent in government and education than their numbers would warrant. Sun Yat-sen, who during that period was the most influential Chinese, was a boyhood convert to Protestantism. Chiang Kai-shek, in control of most of the nation for about a quarter of a century, was baptized, also as a Protestant, after he came to power. Some of the other high officials in his regime have been of that faith. Several of the leading educators of China of the twentieth century have been Christians.

Herein lies one of the adaptations of Christianity to the Chinese environment. For centuries Confucianism had been dominant. It was distinctly this-worldly. It sought to produce an ideal society through men of intelligence and high moral character. In these convictions the intellectuals who administered the realm were nurtured. When, in the twentieth century, Confucianism was weakened, apparently fatally, by the impact of the Occident, that attitude of mind persisted. For a little over a century, from the 1840's to 1950, the Chinese, a proud people, saw their land weak, the victim of foreign invaders, and suffering from corruption and a disintegrating culture. The more thoughtful and high-minded were desperately seeking to regain the nation's independence and to make the country strong and prosperous. From their Confucian heritage they believed that this could come about only through moral regeneration. To many of them Christianity seemed to provide the needed dynamic. Numbers of Protestant missionaries presented it in that light. Missionaries also assisted China in practical ways—introducing modern Western medicine, surgery, public health, forestry, and agricultural techniques. It was for the remaking of China into a strong and prosperous nation that numbers of leading Protestant Chinese saw the chief worth of Christianity. Here was a one-sided view of the Gospel which either missed or tended to minimize its essence.

This misunderstanding of Christianity contributed, although only in a minor way, to the triumph of Communism. Numbers who had been attracted to Christianity as a means of saving China from its weakness thought that they saw in Communism a shorter road to that goal. They either abandoned Christianity outright or sought to bring churches and other Christian organizations to the support of the Communist regime.

There is another and largely opposite side of the Chinese heritage to which many Christians have tended to conform. It is other-worldly, the desire to attain to a blissful immortality beyond the grave. In this lay the main strength of the appeal of the two religions, Buddhism and Taoism, which for centuries had been the chief rivals of Confucianism. Many missionaries, Roman Catholic and Protestant, presented Christianity as the only way of realizing that hope. Numbers of Chinese Christians reinforced that appeal. Indeed, some Protestant movements and leaders which were largely or entirely independent of missionaries stressed that aspect of the Christian faith. As in Buddhism, Taoism, and Confucianism, much emphasis was placed upon the reform of the morals of the individual. To many Christianity became a higher morality.

In both interpretations the wonder of the Gospel, with its distinctive this-worldliness and other-worldliness and its appearance in history in one who is both God and man, and the amazing love, grace, and power of God, has been either only dimly discerned or entirely missed. Some there have been who have appreciated it, but among professing Christians they have probably been a minority. Written as are these lines at a time when the Christians of China are almost entirely cut off from those in the rest of the world, the question arises whether that minority will propagate itself and whether, when physical communications are resumed, the inner vitality will be seen to have persisted and further to have leavened the lump of the nation's life. We do not know.

With Japan we complete our eastward pilgrimage of peoples of "advanced" non-Occidental cultures. In Japan Christianity has been a more recent arrival than in either India or China. It was first introduced, by Roman Catholics, in the sixteenth century. Then, after about half a century of seeming prosperity, severe persecution drove it underground. Not until the 1850's were missionaries again permitted to enter. It was only in 1873 that official persecution of Christians ceased and that the edict boards were removed which declared Christianity to be evil and forbade its acceptance. In the 1930's and during World War II, as a phase of Japanese chauvinism persecution was renewed, but by less violent measures. Partly because it is of more recent introduction, Christianity in Japan is numerically weaker than in China or India. Christians constitute only about one in two hundred of the population.

In Japan the faith has been spread by Russian Orthodox, Roman Catholics, and Protestants. Russian Orthodox have been less numerous than Roman Catholics, and Roman Catholics have not been as numerous as Protestants.

There are three notable features of the response which reflect the adaptation of Christianity to the environment. First, In Japan Christianity is an urban faith. Presumably because missionaries have there chiefly concentrated their efforts, Christians are much more numerous in the rapidly growing industrial and commercial cities than in rural districts. Second, in the cities Christians, and especially Protestants, have been from the middle and professional classes. Why this is so is not quite clear. It may be because missionaries have directed their attention more to those groups. Perhaps it is because those groups, with an education of a partially Western kind, have been more nearly uprooted from the inherited culture and so have been more accessible to a faith from abroad. This, it will be noted, is in striking contrast with the social origins of most of the converts in India. Third, Japanese Christians earlier went farther towards attaining ecclesiastical independence from the churches of the Occident than has been true in any other country. Because of the ecclesiastical structure this end has been more nearly accomplished in Russian Orthodoxy and

Protestantism than in Roman Catholicism. True to its genius, the latter is still under the direction of the Vatican. Early in the twentieth century Russian Orthodox and Protestant Japanese Christians had made great progress in attaining the goal of self-government and self-support, and in the 1930's under the exigencies of the international situation all the bishops and other chief administrative officers of the Roman Catholic, Russian Orthodox, and Protestant churches were Japanese.

In Japan the repercussions of Christianity outside the churches have been unlike those in India and China. We have noted the very marked influences in both lands, although different in each, outside the Christian communities. In Japan these have been chiefly seen in the observance of Christmas. That festival has become an occasion for celebrations far beyond Christian circles. In the large cities it has become almost universal. To be sure, it has been commercialized and secularized, but something of its meaning must have reached multitudes whom otherwise the Gospel has touched slightly or not at all. In Japan, too, a "no-church" Christianity has arisen from contact with Protestants. Its founder was Uchimura. It has no baptism or Eucharist and no formal organization. Those who are connected with it are largely intellectuals. Through Bible study and lectures they have contact with Christian teaching, but they are bound by no creed. Yet those of this fellowship are more frankly attached to Jesus than are most of the "invisible Christians" of India—those who are influenced by Christ but have never been baptized or broken with Hinduism. They are not numerous but many of them are prominent in their communities.

CHAPTER V

The Issues in Retrospect

Now that we have completed our brief survey of the contemporary scene, what can be said in summary? How has Christianity responded to the world of our day? How has that world responded to Christianity?

We must again and again remind ourselves that Christianity is not identical with the Gospel. What we call Christianity is part of the human response to the Gospel. Therefore, in it is much of human sin and lack of understanding. In degrees which vary with each Christian individual and group, these have been in part overcome by the Gospel. The Church, "the blessed company of all faithful people," is made up of forgiven sinners. But the sinners, although forgiven, are still sinners. Like Paul, they have not yet attained perfection nor are they already perfect. At best, as did he, they are pressing on towards the goal of the high calling of God in Christ Jesus. To put it in another way, the Church is *in via* but is not yet *in patria*. Often the caricature of the Gospel presented by the churches which are the partial embodiment of the Church has led conscientious souls to reject the Gospel. Or, in their reaction against Christianity as they have seen it in the churches, they take certain elements from the Gospel and ignore others. Thus in their turn they distort, perhaps even more drastically, what

God has offered in Christ. It is thought-provoking even if frustrating to speculate what course the development of Karl Marx, and, in consequence, of much of recent history, would have taken if that sensitive spirit had come into close and continuing friendship with a representative of the Gospel who commanded at once his intellectual and his spiritual and moral respect. Would he, for example, have arrived at other conclusions if, during the years when he was eating out his heart in poverty in the slums of London, nourishing burning indignation against the fruits of callous capitalism which he saw about him and regarding the Church of England as a bulwark of the order against which he was protesting, he had known intimately his older contemporary, John Frederick Denison Maurice, who in another part of London was seeking to bring Christian principles to bear on the kind of society against which Marx raged, or if he had become acquainted with a younger contemporary, William Booth, who in those very slums in the last two decades of Marx's life, through the Christian Mission and then the Salvation Army, was attempting, in another fashion, a Christian solution?

However, is not the caricaturing and even the perversion of the Gospel by those bearing the name of Christian the risk that God takes? Is it not part of the wonder of the Gospel as it is seen in the Incarnation and on Calvary? Is not here the inescapable way of love in the face of evil and of man's pride and self-will? Does not history show the seeming foolishness of God to be wiser than men and the apparent weakness of God to be stronger than men? Could He have brought to birth sons in any other way? Does not the emergence of sons of God in increasing numbers and in all races and cultures demonstrate His wisdom and His power?

It may be that a corollary to this last paragraph is in the prominence of Protestantism in the past century and the current scene. Even a casual perusal of the preceding pages will disclose the fact that of the major forms of the faith it is chiefly from Protestantism that there has come the stimulus which has given rise to the many movements and variants, some within Christianity and some outside it, several of which we have noted. Only a slight number have issued from the Orthodox Churches. More have come from the Roman Catholic Church. Far more have sprung from Protestantism. We need here to remind ourselves of only a few of them.

In his boyhood Marx was a Christian, and a Lutheran rather than a Roman Catholic. The new way of bringing Christians together, the Ecumenical Movement, is from Protestantism. In the shaping of the distinctive forms which Christianity is taking in the United States Protestantism has been the chief determining religious factor. From Protestantism have come most of the variants of Christianity among "primitive" peoples, such as the Bantu sects in South Africa and the prophet movements in other parts of Africa. It was from Protestantism that the Brahmo Samaj and the Servants of India Society drew their inspiration, and it was through that form of the faith that Gandhi gained most of his knowledge of Christianity. The contributions from Christianity to the T'ai P'ings, to Sun Yat-sen, and to most of the other leaders in modern China who were indebted to that religion came through Protestantism. In Japan the "no-Church Christianity" of Uchimura arose from contacts with Protestantism.

Why this prominence of Protestantism as a source of these movements? May it not be because of the greater freedom in Protestantism with its possibility of new expressions, some of which may depart far from the central core of the faith? The Orthodox Churches have been too subordinate to the state, too much committed to inflexible dogma, and in their spiritual life too dominated by monasticism with its retreat from the world to be the source of marked variations. They continue to produce saints of a monastic kind, but not for two centuries or more have major heresies come from them. The Roman Catholic Church has abounding vitality. It is active in spreading the faith among non-Western peoples. It is rich in works of charity and in disciplines of prayer and of the ascetic life. Yet it is less and less flexible and more and more under the authoritarian and autocratic direction of the Pope. The distinctive beliefs which separate Protestantism from the other major wings of Christianity are salvation by faith and the priesthood of all believers. An essential concomitant is the right and the duty of individual judgment such as Luther exercised when, before the Diet of Worms in the presence of the Emperor and the lords spiritual and temporal of the Holy Roman Empire, he declared that he could not repudiate what he had written unless convinced by Scripture and plain reason. Increasingly Protestantism has tended to live up to these principles. As critics have often pointed out, they are dangerous. Yet more nearly than any other form of the faith Protestantism reflects the outcome of the act of God in sending His Son to be born in great humility as a helpless infant and then, after a brief public ministry, to be crucified on a Roman cross. It is this seeming weakness, not protected by institutional authority or physical force, which permits departures from the Gospel in the name of the Gospel and which finds freest course in Protestantism.

This does not mean that Protestantism as we know it is the final form of the faith. Indeed, if it is true to its genius it will not be. Other forms will issue from it. What they will be no one ought confidently to predict.

Yet it is important and highly significant that through Protestantism there have come movements, apparently still young, experimental, and in novel guise, for bringing all Christians together in an inclusive fellowship. Moreover, these movements have had their origin in efforts to spread the Christian faith. It is fitting that in the 1950's their leaders issued "a call to mission and unity." That summons, too, is part of the response of Christianity to our world. In a day when time-distances are continuing to shrink and all mankind has become a neighbourhood, even though a tragically quarrelsome neighbourhood, if they are to be true to the Gospel Christians must seek to realize in a global fashion that unity of love among themselves which is of the essence of their faith and for which their Lord prayed on the night in which he was betrayed, and must strive to make disciples of all the nations, teaching them to observe all things which he commanded, including that love of Christians one for the other which he described as "new." After nineteen centuries it is still "new," for it is still far from being fully realized. It has never been more urgently needed than now.

That unity of love, permitting as it must great diversity, can emerge best out of Protestantism, for by its very genius that branch of the faith encourages variety.

Moreover, in the past century and a half the mission of the Church has been pushed more vigorously by Protestantism than by any other wing of the faith. Proportionately Christianity has spread more rapidly through Protestantism than through the Orthodox Churches or even the Roman Catholic Church. From being a strictly regional faith, confined to Northwestern Europe and a few colonies from that area in the Western Hemisphere, on the fringes of Africa, and in South and East Asia, it has become global, represented by growing constituencies in almost every tribe and nation. In the several ecumenical bodies which are springing from it, Protestantism is both seeking to present the Gospel to all men and reaching out to draw into new expressions of unity not only those baptized into its fellowship but also Christians of other branches of the faith, and that without sacrificing their allegiance to these communions.

Will Protestantism continue to be true to the Gospel, that core of Christianity without which responses of that religion to various environments are denatured or captured by demonic forces? No one ought to be confident in his reply. Protestantism faces at least two dangers. One is that, with its emphasis upon the right and the duty of individual judgment it will gradually abandon the heart of the faith which has come to it from pre-Protestant Christianity. This is what many Roman Catholics predict. Here and there that prediction seems to have been verified by the event, notably in several of the movements to which we have called attention. The other danger, and one to which some communions have fallen victim, is that in reacting against this danger Protestantism will seek to safeguard the faith by an arid, authoritarian dogmatism in which the spirit is all but quenched by a belligerent attempt to hold fast to the letter.

Yet in spite of these dangers and numerous examples which prove that they are real, Protestantism continues to be vital, to grow, and by its fruits to show that through it the Gospel still finds channels in which it flows, transformingly, into the world. We who have been nurtured in the Gospel through one or another of the Protestant communions have the responsibility and the high privilege of seeing that these channels remain unclogged. By allowing ourselves to be judged continually by the Word of God as it is in the Scriptures, the Incarnation, the life and teachings of Jesus, the Crucifixion, the Resurrection, the risen and ever-living Christ, and the witness of the Spirit in the ensuing centuries, and by humbly and confidently accepting in faith the amazing grace of God in Jesus Christ, we can trust God so to use us and our always imperfect witness in such fashion that the Gospel will continue to be the power of God unto salvation.

INDEX

Set in Intertype Baskerville
Format by Marguerite Swanton
Manufactured by The Haddon Craftsmen, Inc.
Published by Harper & Brothers, *New York*